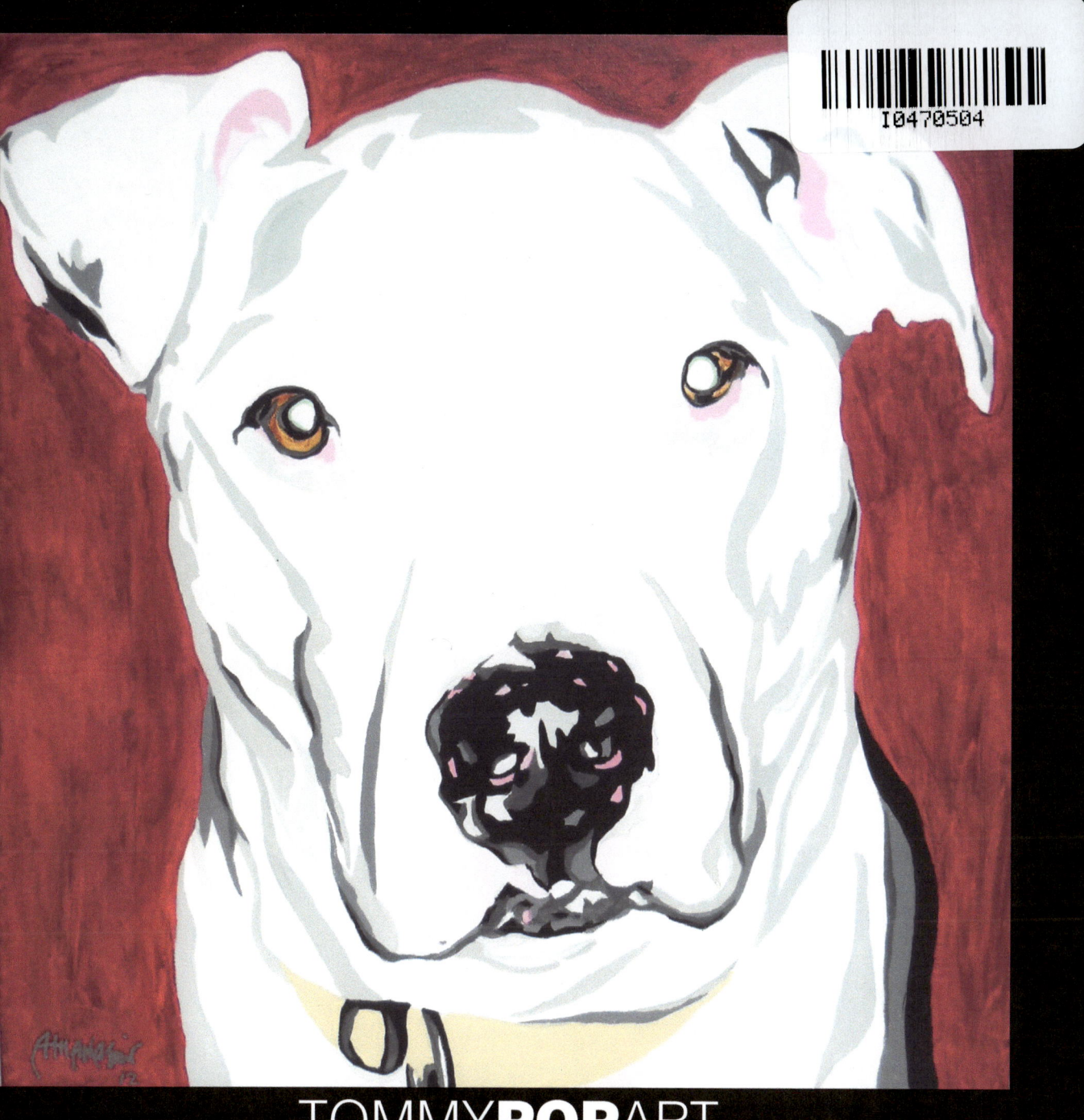

TOMMY**POP**ART
The First 6 Years: 2009-2015

Dedicated to
Sharon,
Mom, & Dad

The Art of Tommy Pop Art

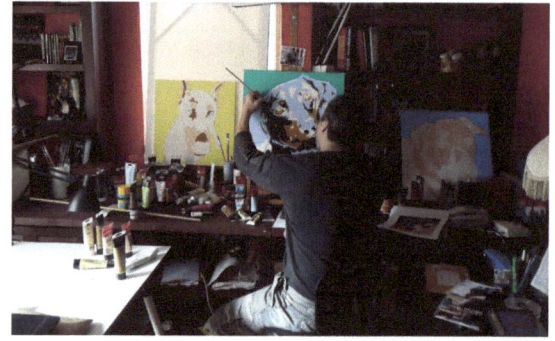

The First 6 Years: 2009-2015

Written, Illustrated, and Designed by Thomas Andrew Athanasiou
Edited by Sharon Athanasiou

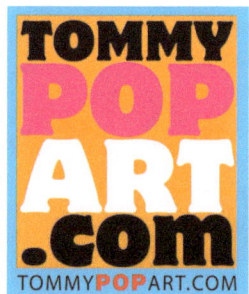

www.TommyPopArt.com

Like us on Facebook: Tommy Pop Art

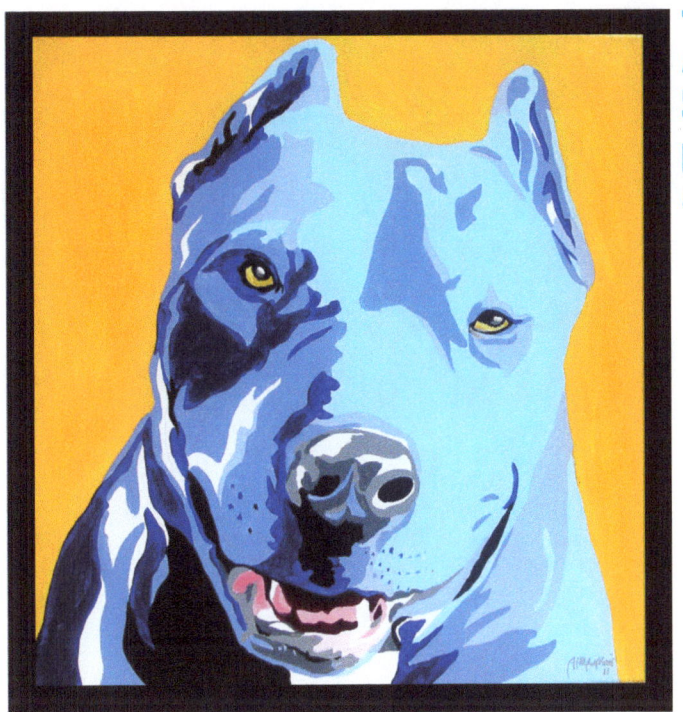

The
Art
of
Tommy
Pop
Art

On The Cover:
SMOKEY 2
original

TOMMY**POP**ART
CONTENTS

The First
6 Years:
2009-2015

6 forward

8 in**the**beginning...

10 pop**pets**

54 personal**art**

56 pitbull**shirt**.com

58 children's**books**

60 ...the**grand**finale**?**

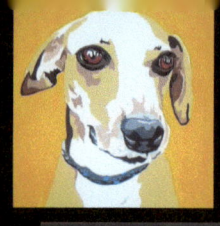

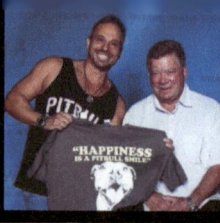

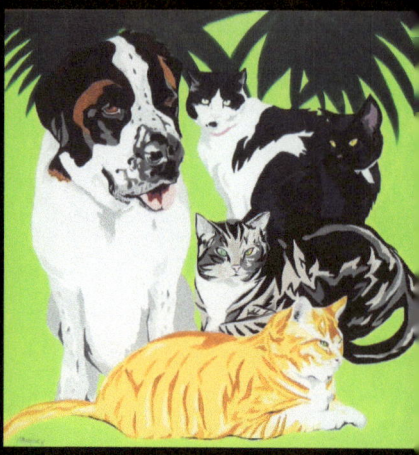

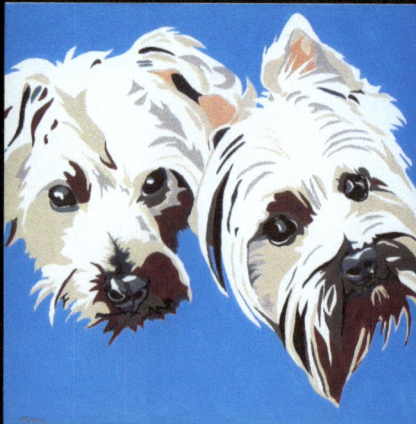

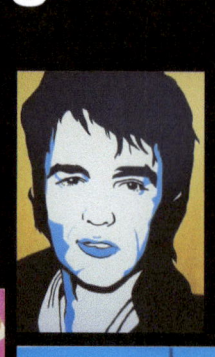

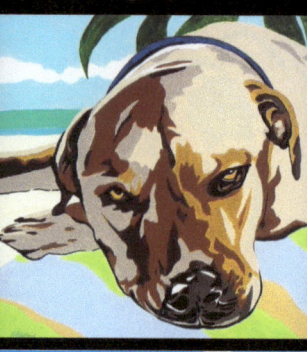

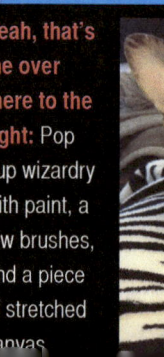

Yeah, that's me over there to the right: Pop pup wizardry with paint, a few brushes, and a piece of stretched canvas.

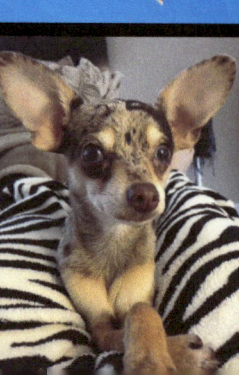

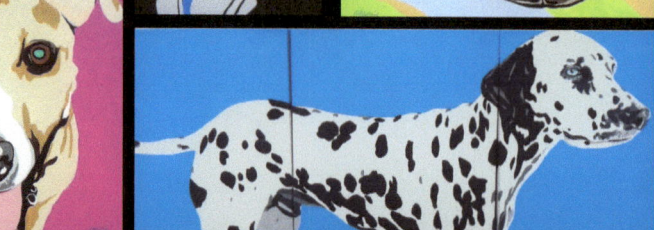

TOMMY**POP**ART

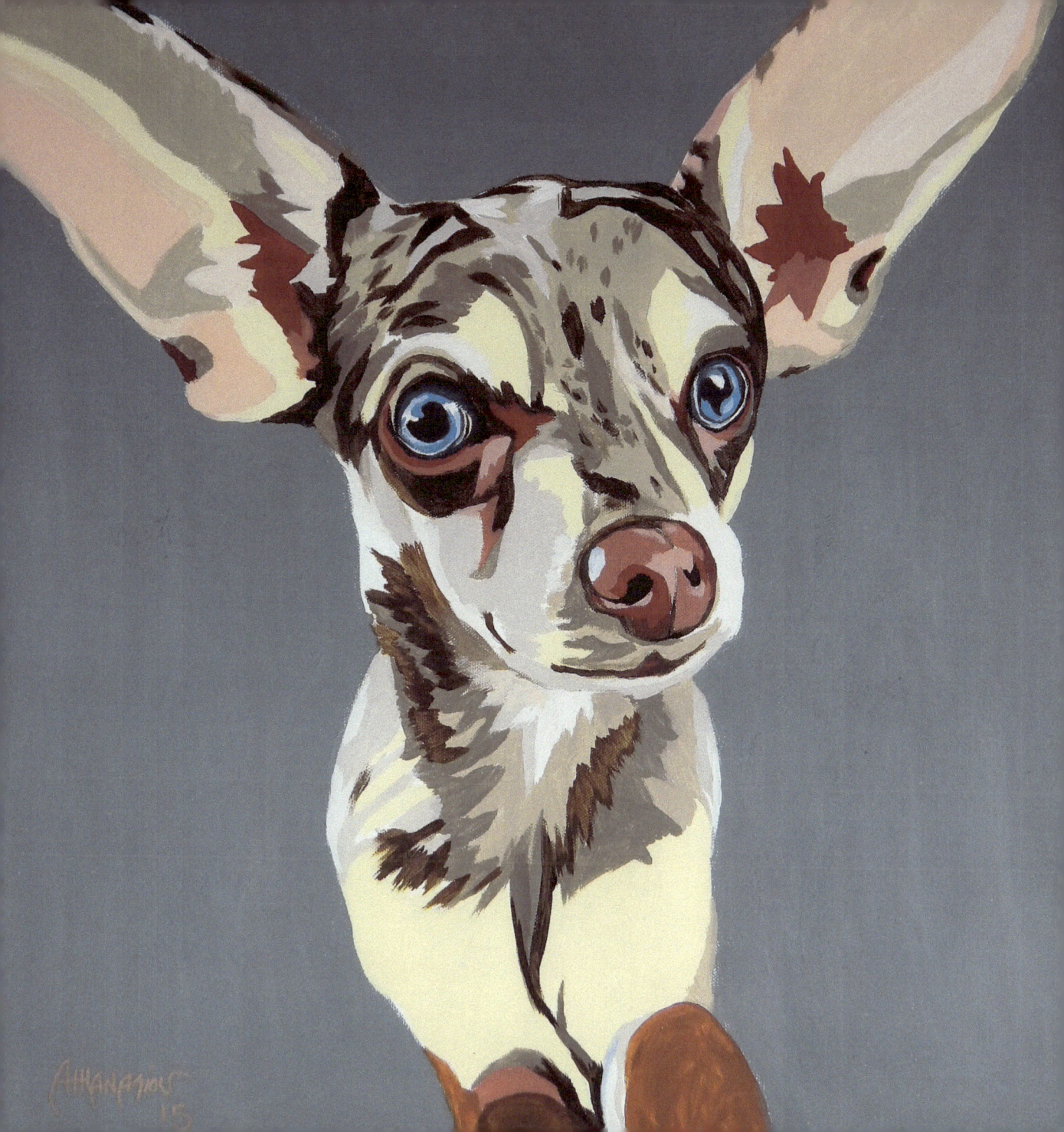

TOMMY**POP**ART
FORWORD

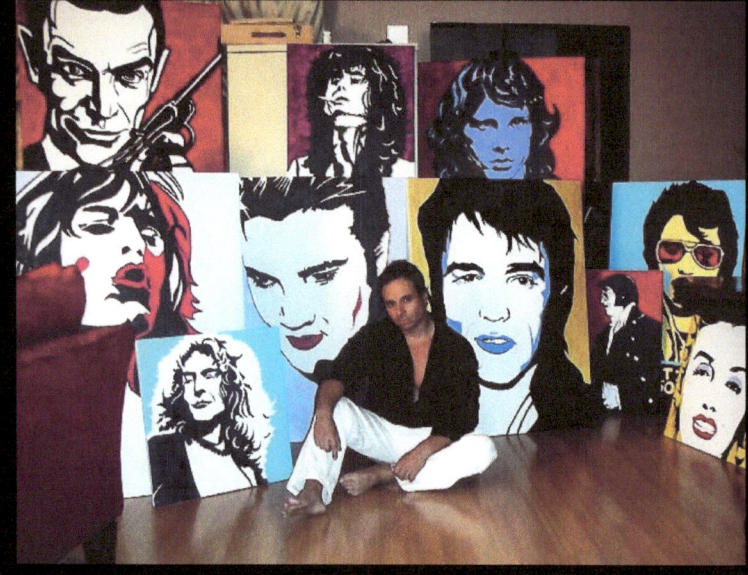

Why pop art? Why not do the stuff you were trained for, like realistic oil painting illustrations? What's weird is, I've always been attracted to the simple design formula of art. If you can make magic happen with a few shapes and colors, you've got it mastered! So, the next question, "Why 'Tommy Pop Art'?" I guess it comes back to the answer above: Just keeping it simple. Tommy does Pop Art.

What I have gathered here from the archives are the majority of all my Pop Art Pet portaits from the last six years. I've also thrown in some of the other ingredients that chronicle the rest of my achievements, including some never-before-seen personal pop paintings from 2008.

I hope you enjoy the book. Maybe it will inspire you to just "give it a shot" and see where an idea takes you.

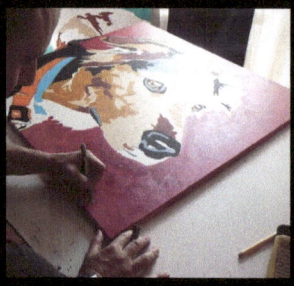

Clockwise: A burst of creative energy. Tommy in his studio 2008; Signing a freshly-painted portrait; In the studio with the Boss. A commissioned **Bruce Springstee**n portrait; Hey, you wanna buy a painting? Tommy's first showing at a 3-day dog show event in Miami. Paintings commissioned: 0.

Tommy Athanasiou
October 2015

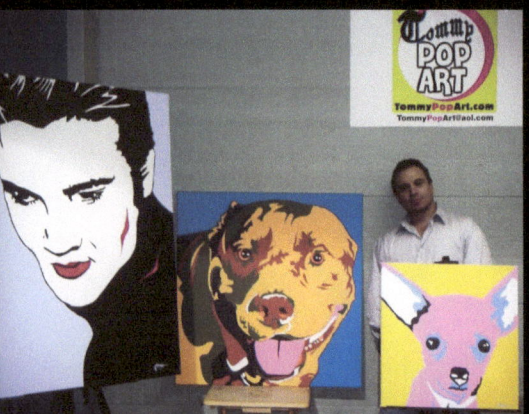

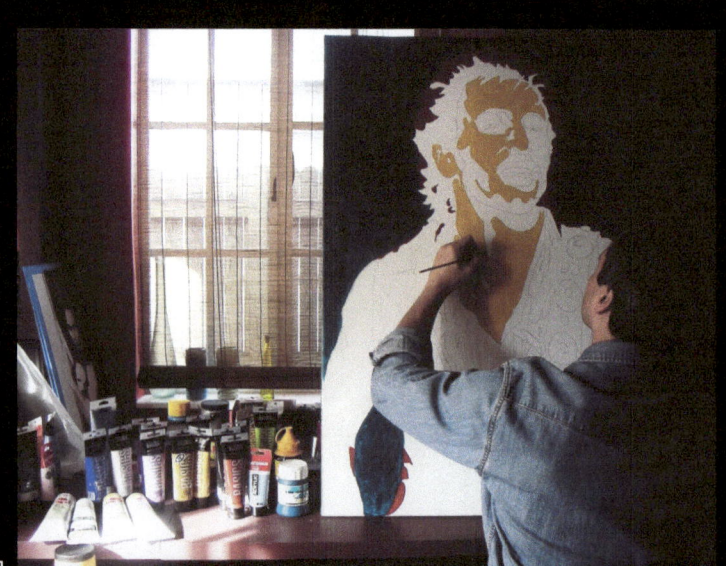

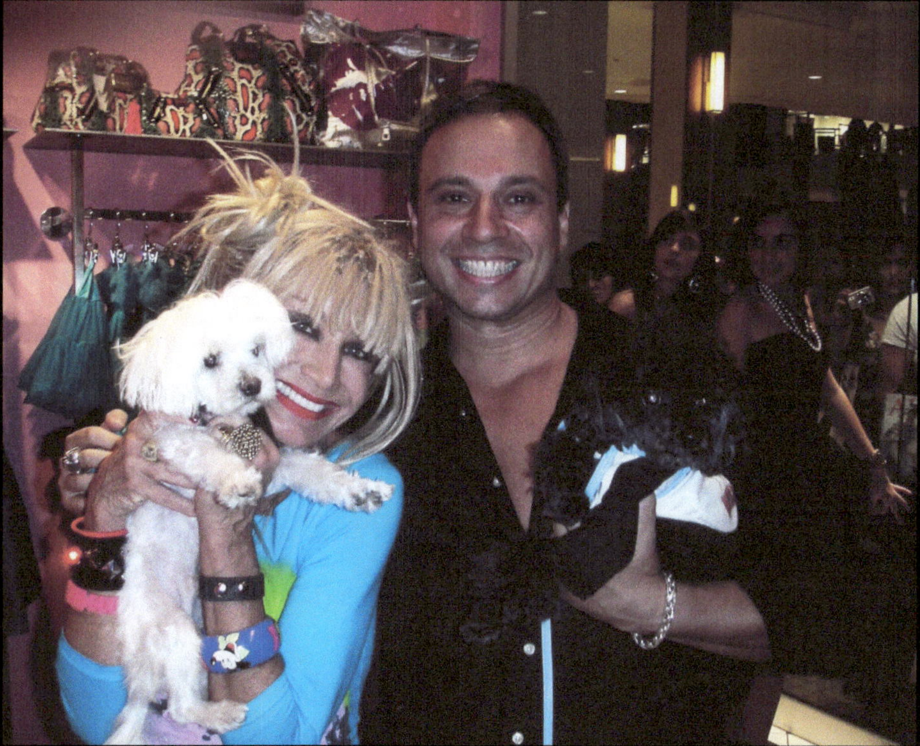

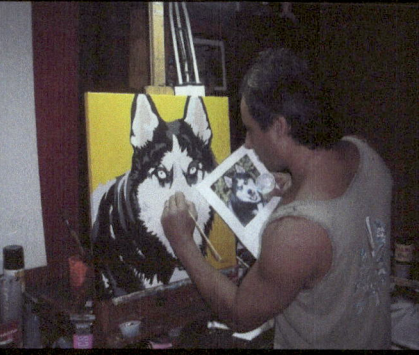

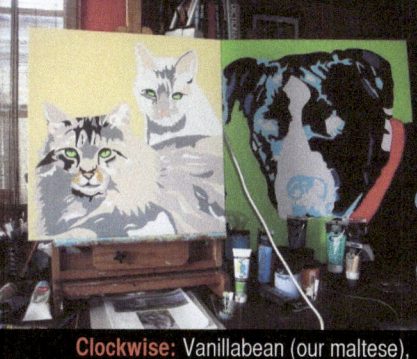

Clockwise: Vanillabean (our maltese), legendary fashion designer **Betsey Johnson**, Tommy, and Fluffernutter (our poodle), at a function in one of her stores; It's all in the minute details when it comes to the eyes — the last piece in rendering the puzzle; There are usually 2 or more paintings going at all times; A painted urn for Kaos; Knocking it out clear over the fence. 4 pop paintings of a clients dogs viewed pop style; **Cesar Millan** and Tommy with his *Peanut The Pitbull* Children's book that was donated for a Cesar Millan Foundation silent auction charity.

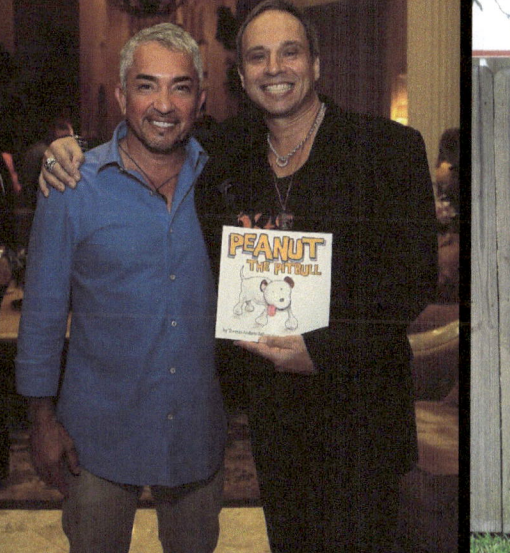

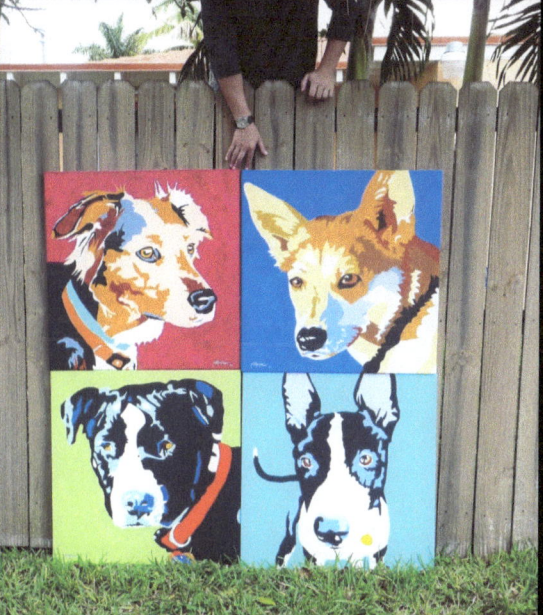

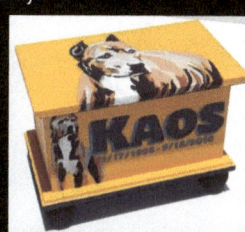

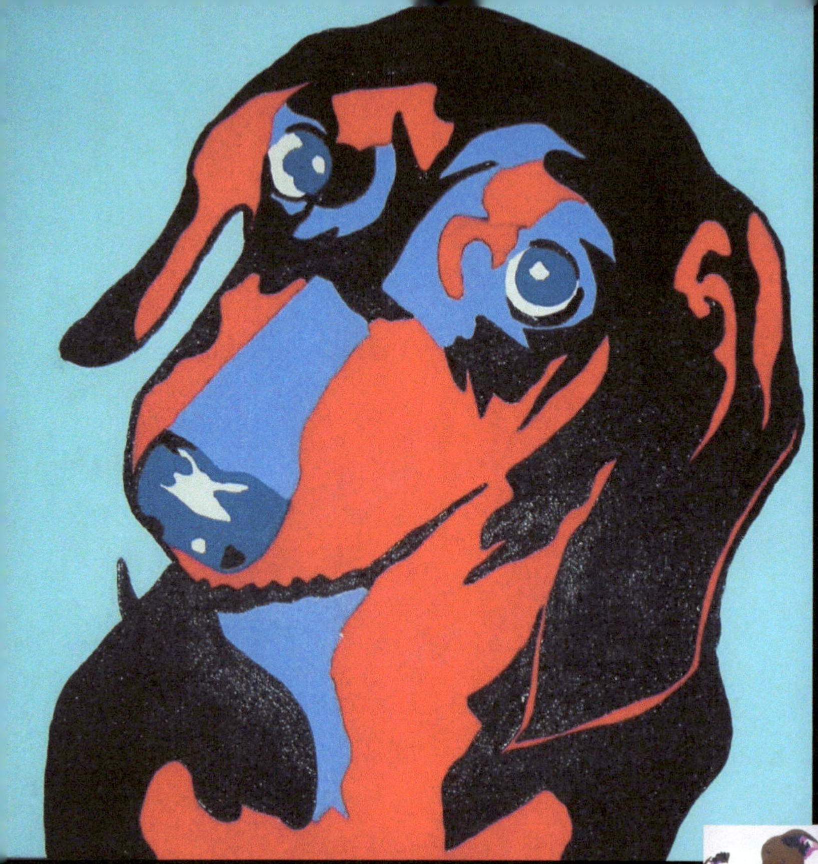

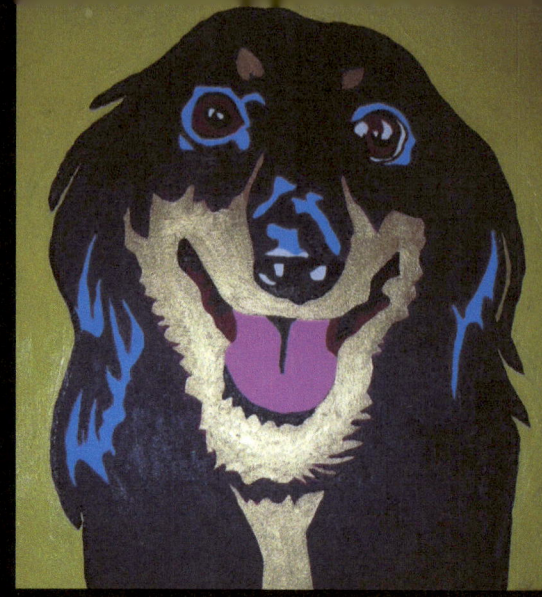

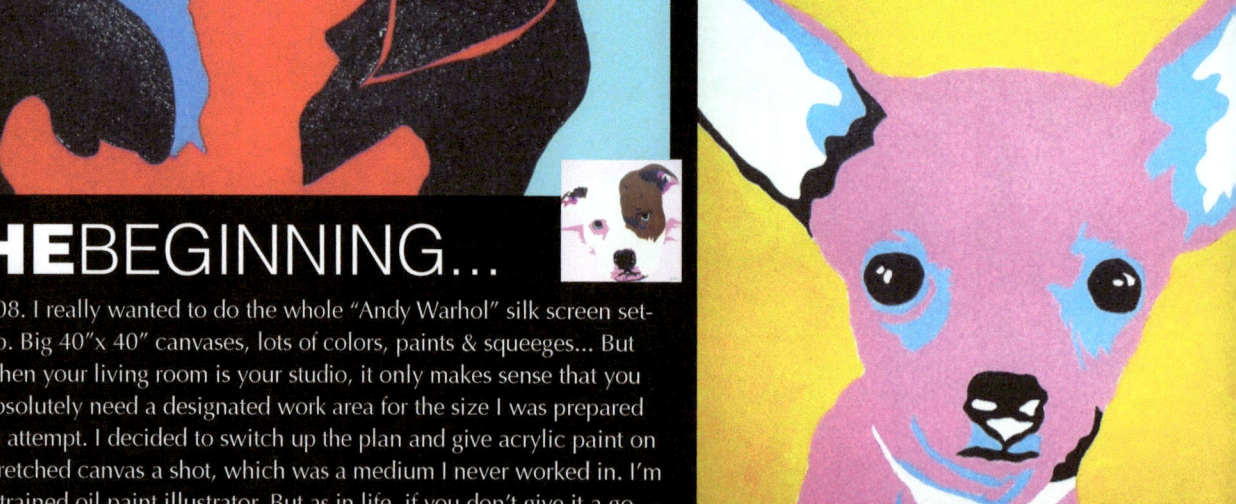

N**THE**BEGINNING…

2008. I really wanted to do the whole "Andy Warhol" silk screen set-up. Big 40"x 40" canvases, lots of colors, paints & squeeges… But when your living room is your studio, it only makes sense that you absolutely need a designated work area for the size I was prepared to attempt. I decided to switch up the plan and give acrylic paint on stretched canvas a shot, which was a medium I never worked in. I'm a trained oil paint illustrator. But as in life, if you don't give it a go, you'll never know. The concept was there; it was all about retaining the "original" pop art structure. The first creations were my personal paintings. Next up are the early 2009 commissioned originals (some are on this page), but it really kicked into gear with Smokey The Pitbull (on the next page). He was a beautiful abused dog whose rescuer needed money for medical treatment. I decided to do-nate a painting for an auction benefitting him, and I got noticed by fellow art lovers who wanted their pets painted too. That's when the work really started to come in. Instant karma's gonna get you!

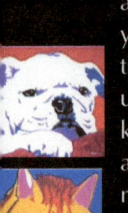

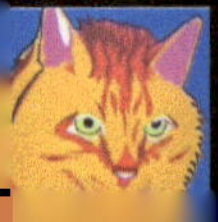

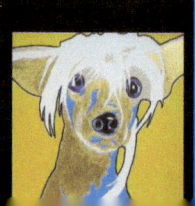

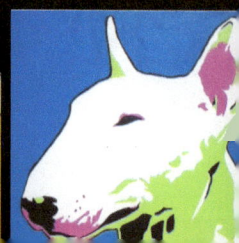

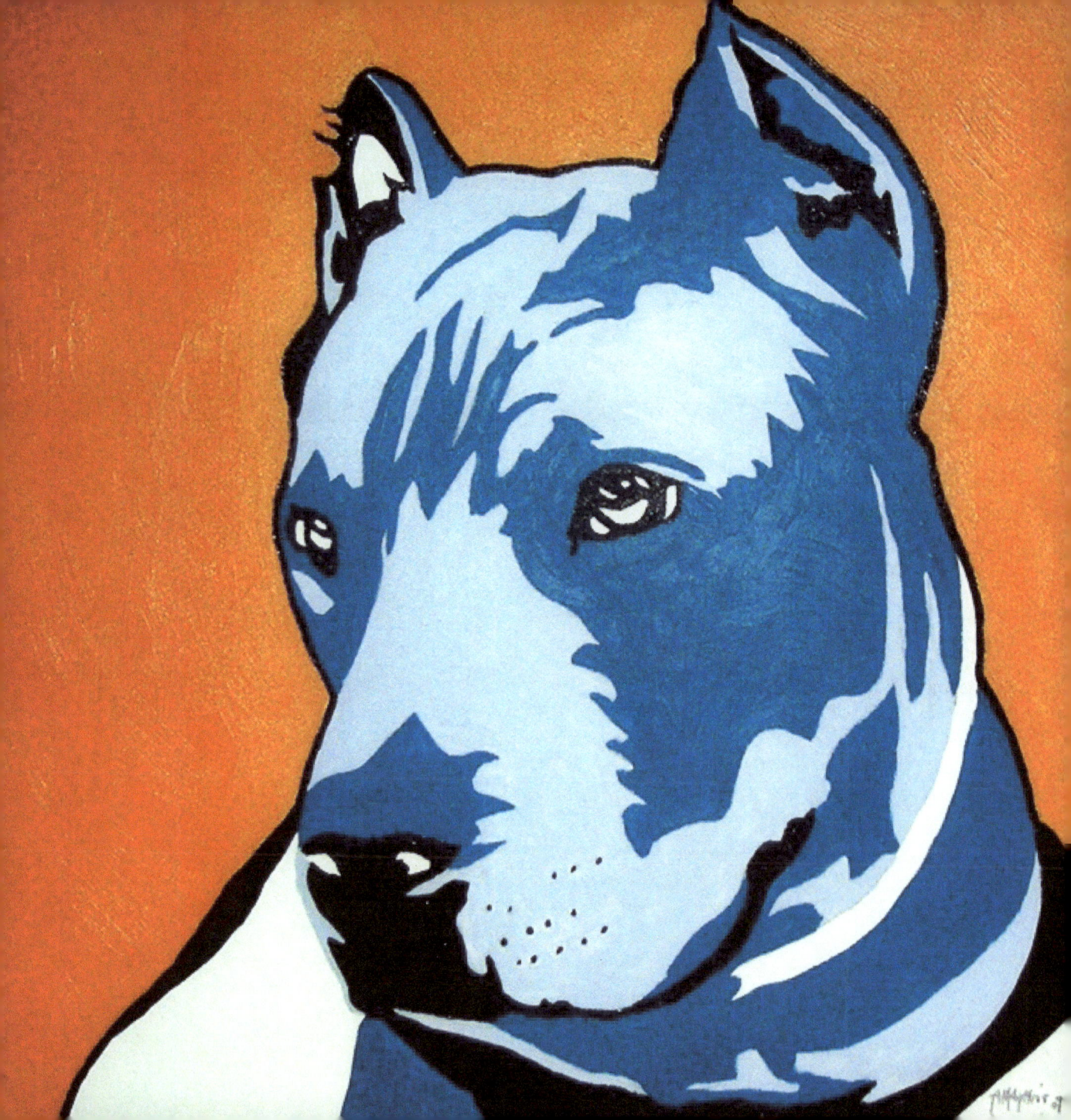

POP**PETS**

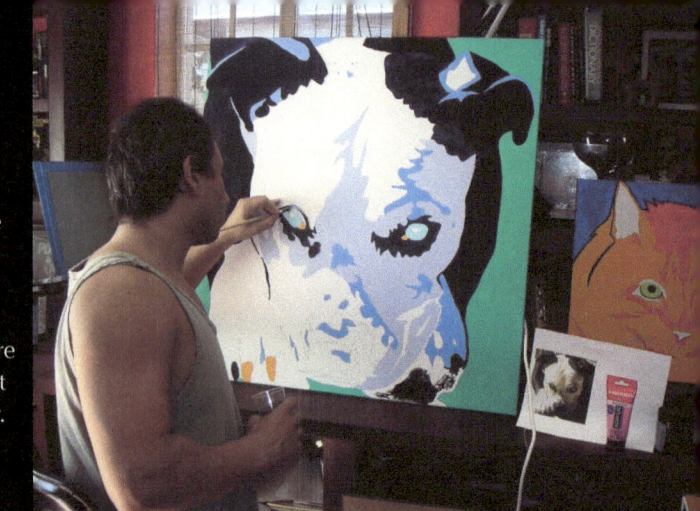

The Tommy Pop Art style was starting to emerge and this rockstar (these 2 pages) from California named Romeo definitely accomplished that. Every painting that followed had that certain edge, the added shadows, and the soulful eyes. This section of the book focuses on the pets. I shuffled up the deck, so you'll see 6 years worth of portraits side by side. My portaits range from the smallest at 20" x 20", to 50" x 60", and everything in between. Another thing you might notice is that most are square. This coming from the Andy Warhol concept that all of this art is interchangeable. Ah, pop art philosophy. To me it just looks cool, like an album cover.

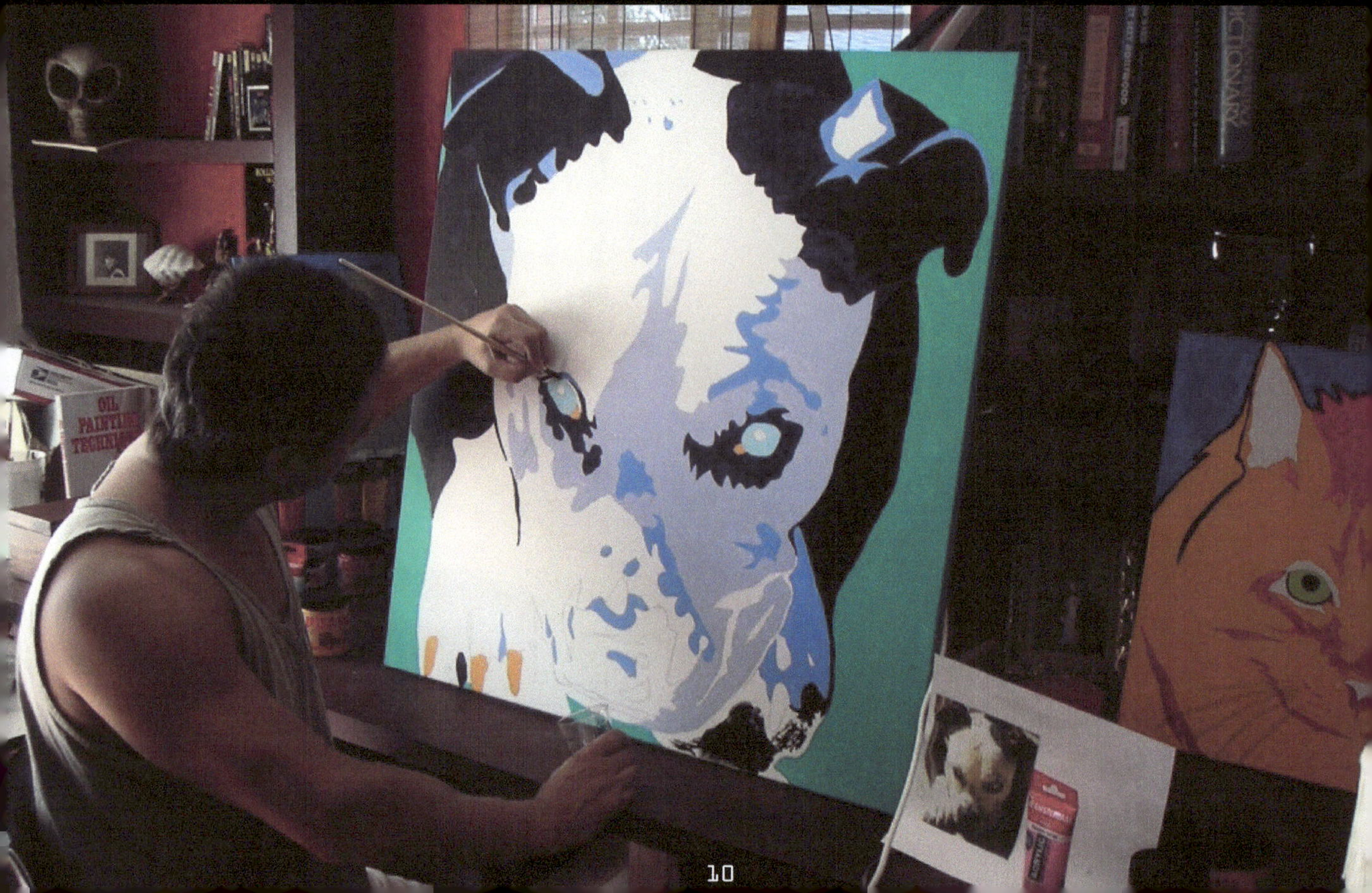

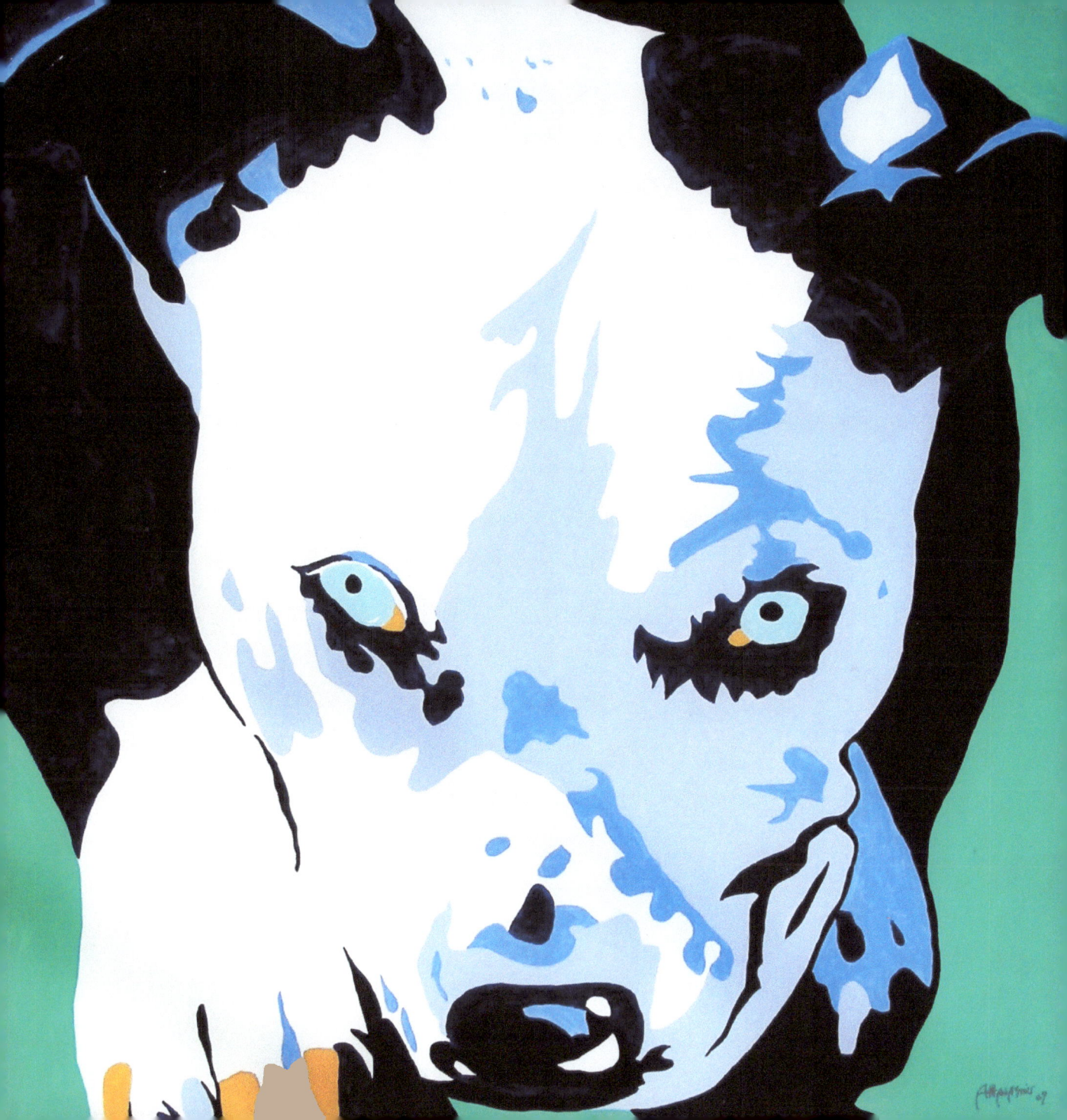

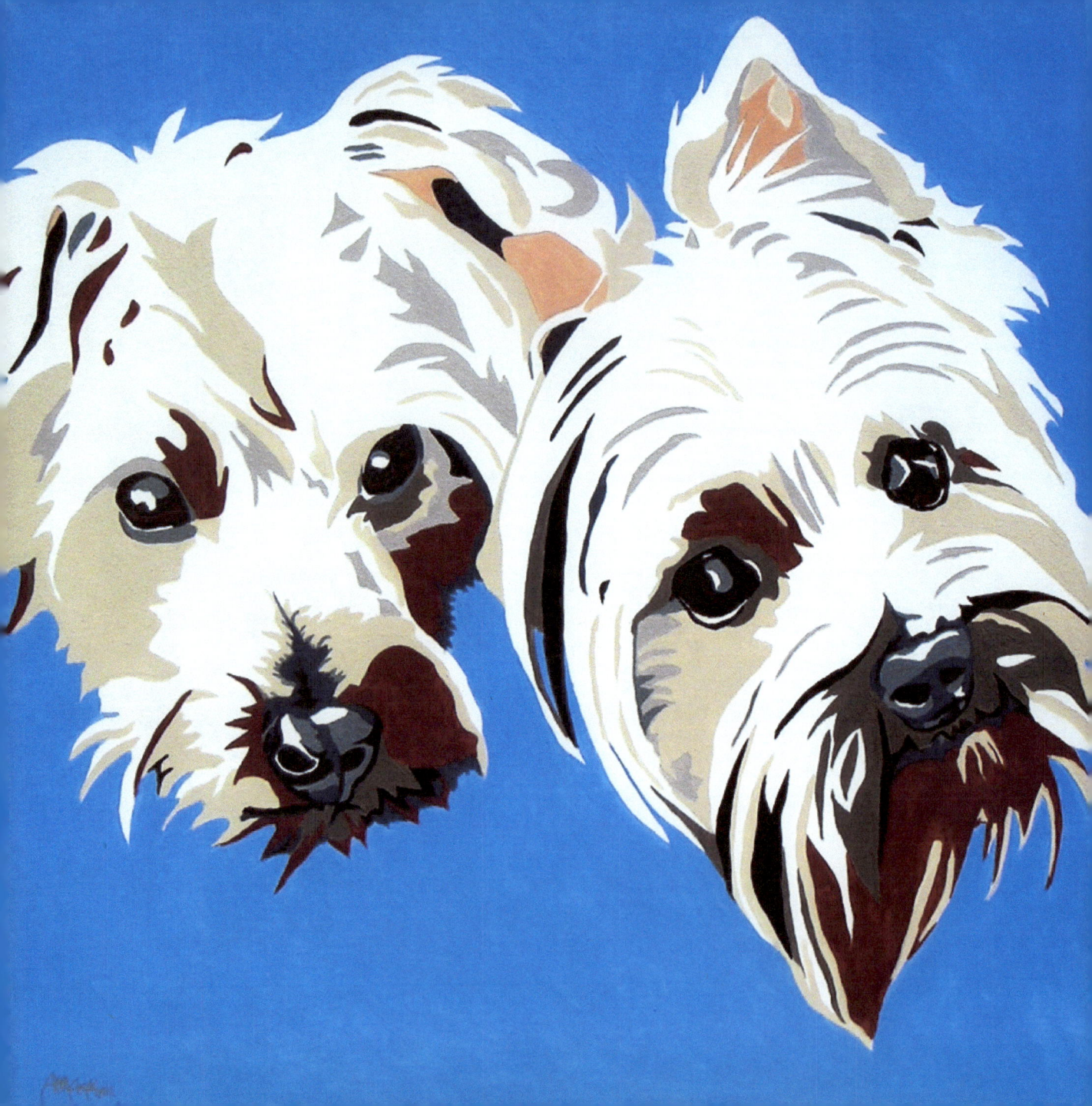

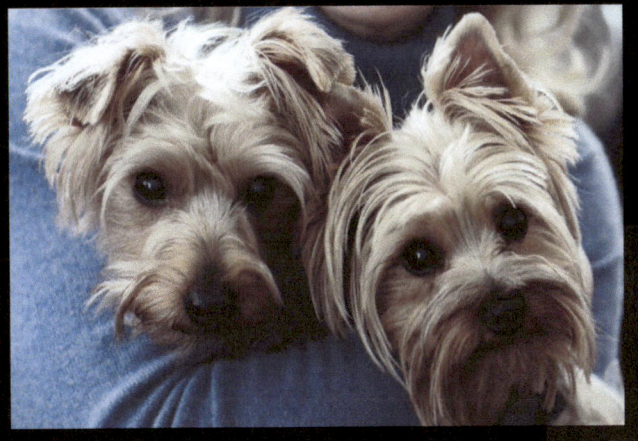

Start To Finish: So how does a portrait begin? With a great picture like the one above. Perfect lighting, nice colors (chosen by the client), and great shadows. This portrait was the begining of the "natural look" (utlilizing the actual color of the pet, while adding a vivid background, which eventually became the most requested style). The picture is then rendered with pencil on a prestretched canvas. I always start with the background first (see right) when it's time to paint and try to get most of the larger elements done before we tackle the minute details, which, most of the time, are hand-mixed custom colors. Meaning, you get one shot to paint that area. It's almost impossible to get that same color again.

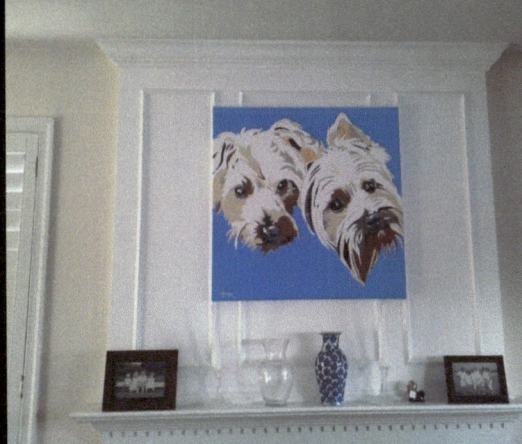

Completed and hanging over the fireplace. How elegant is that?

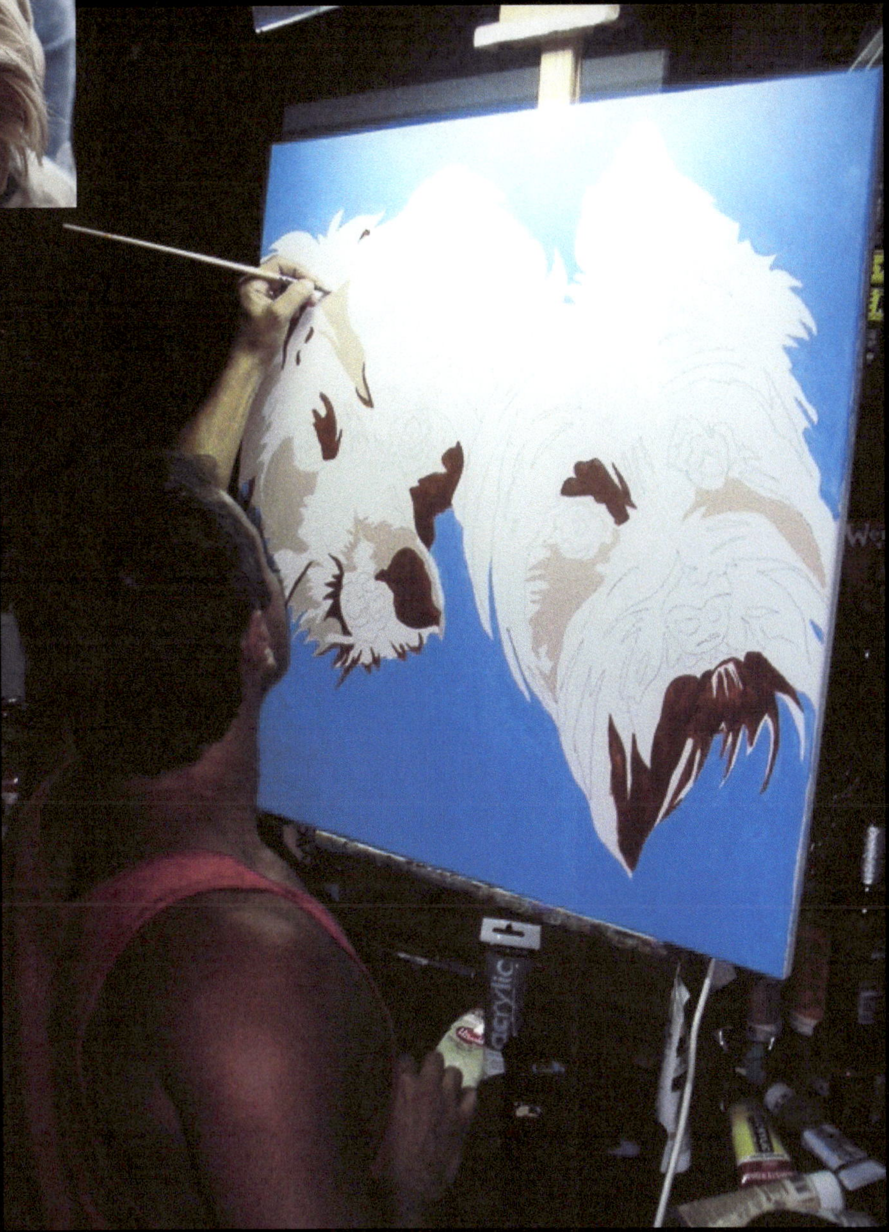

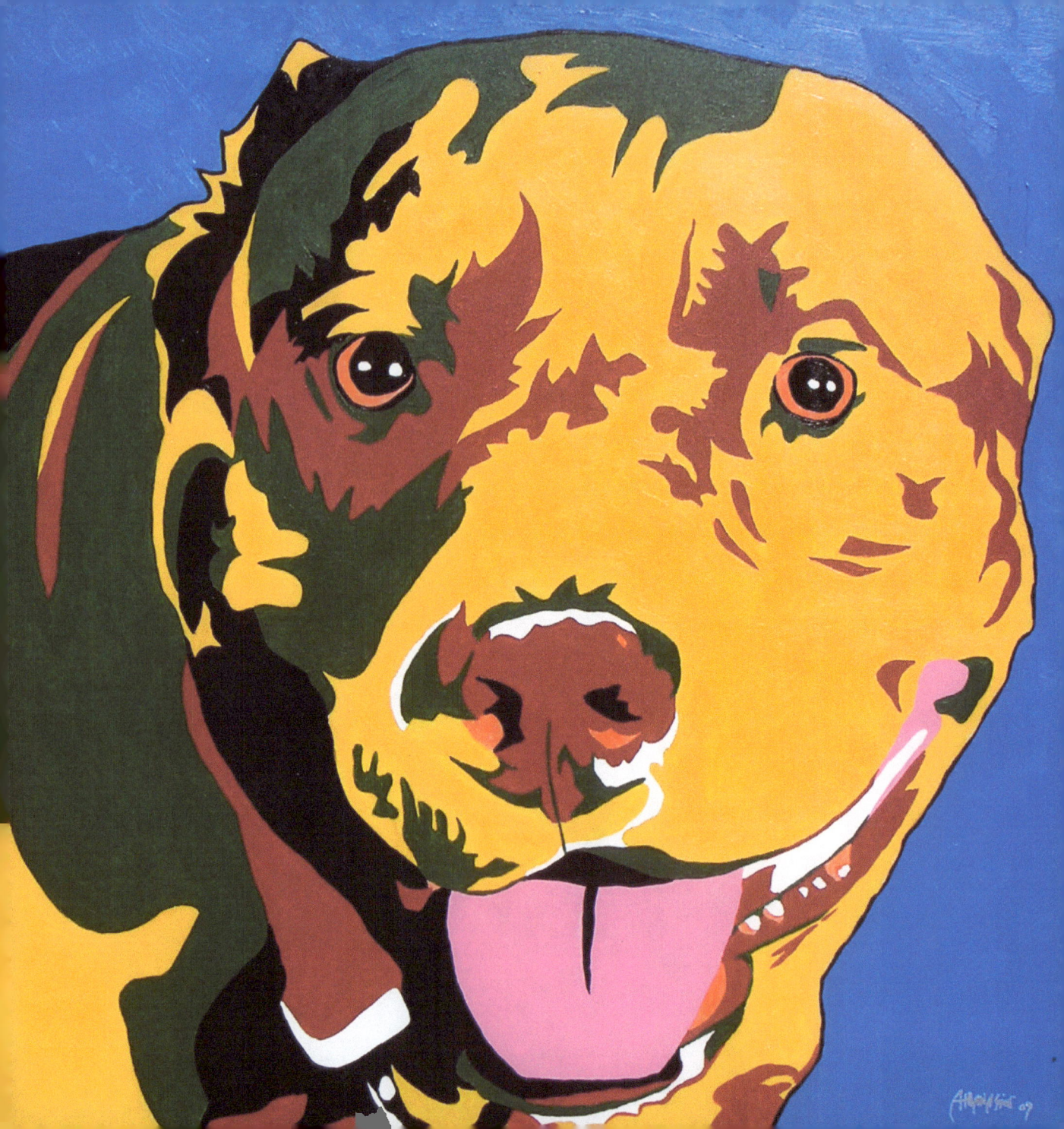

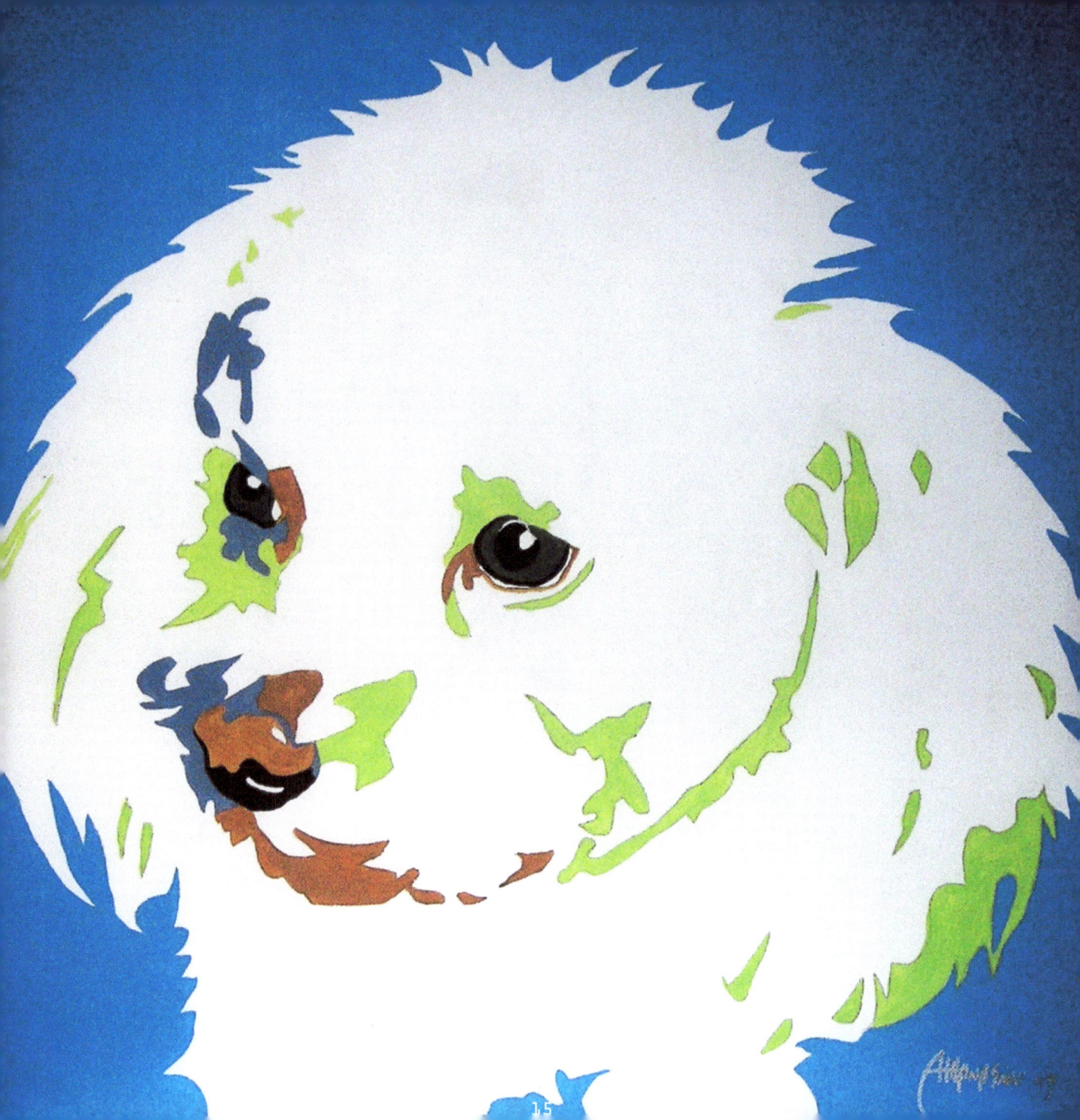

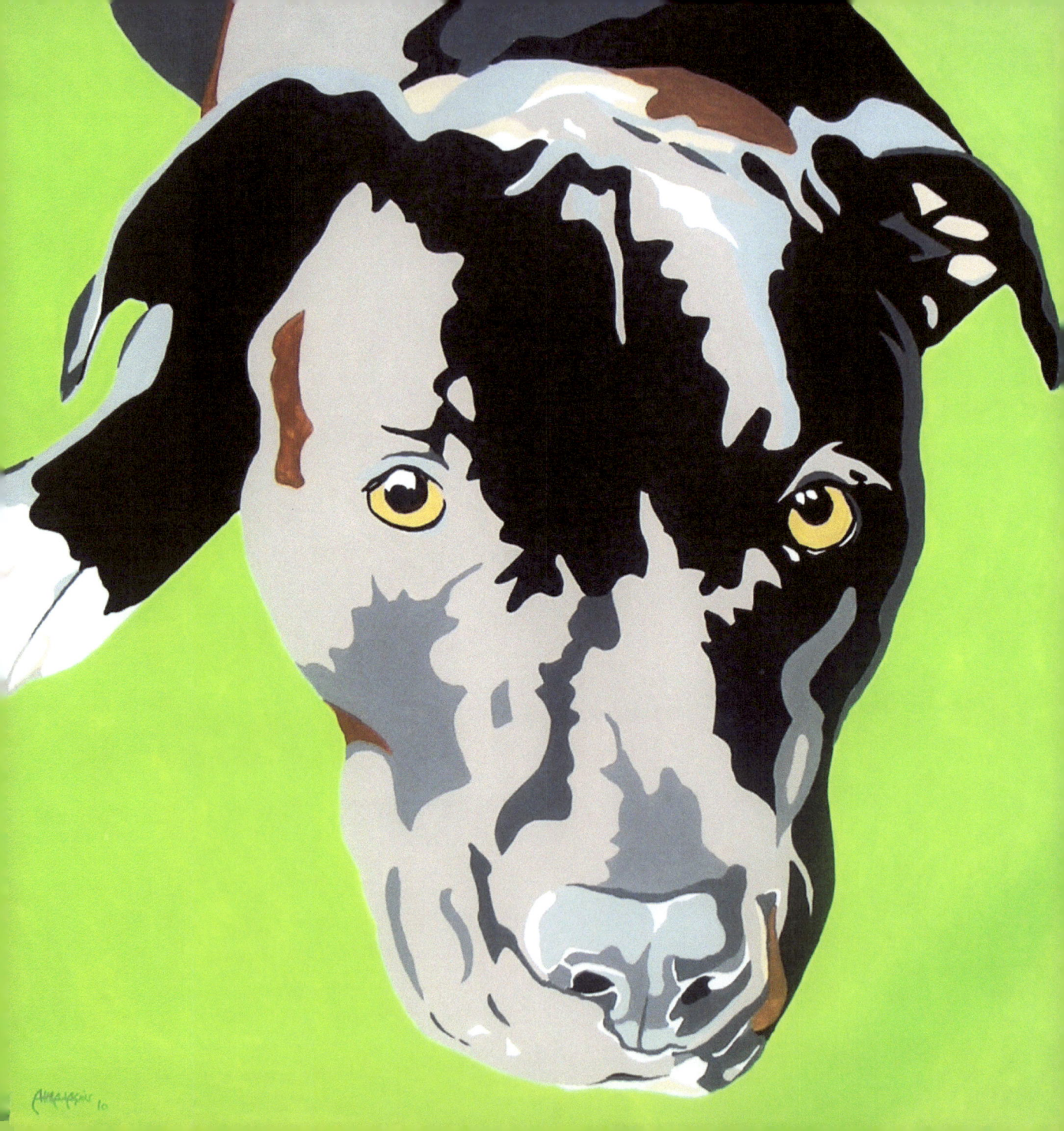

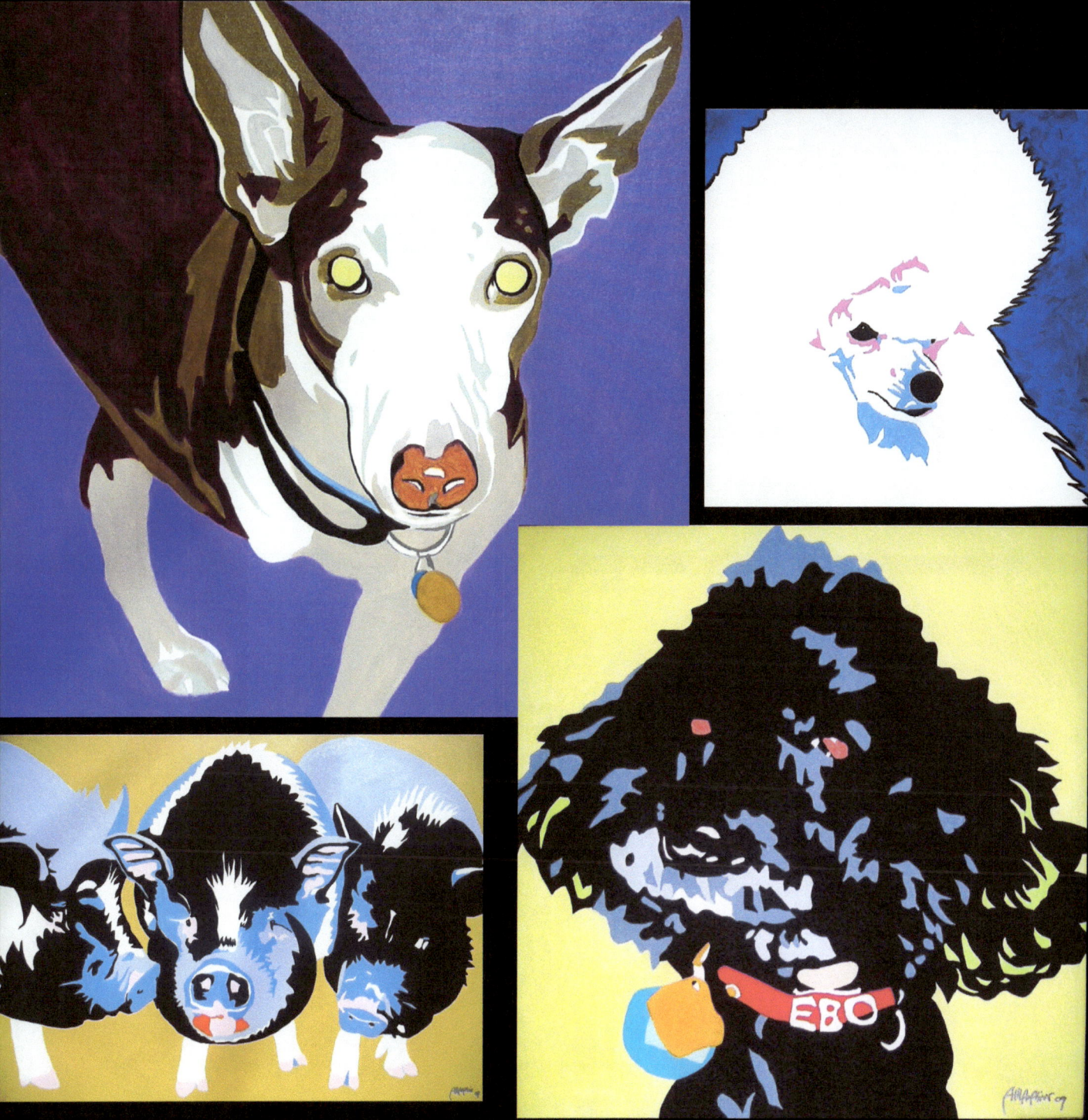

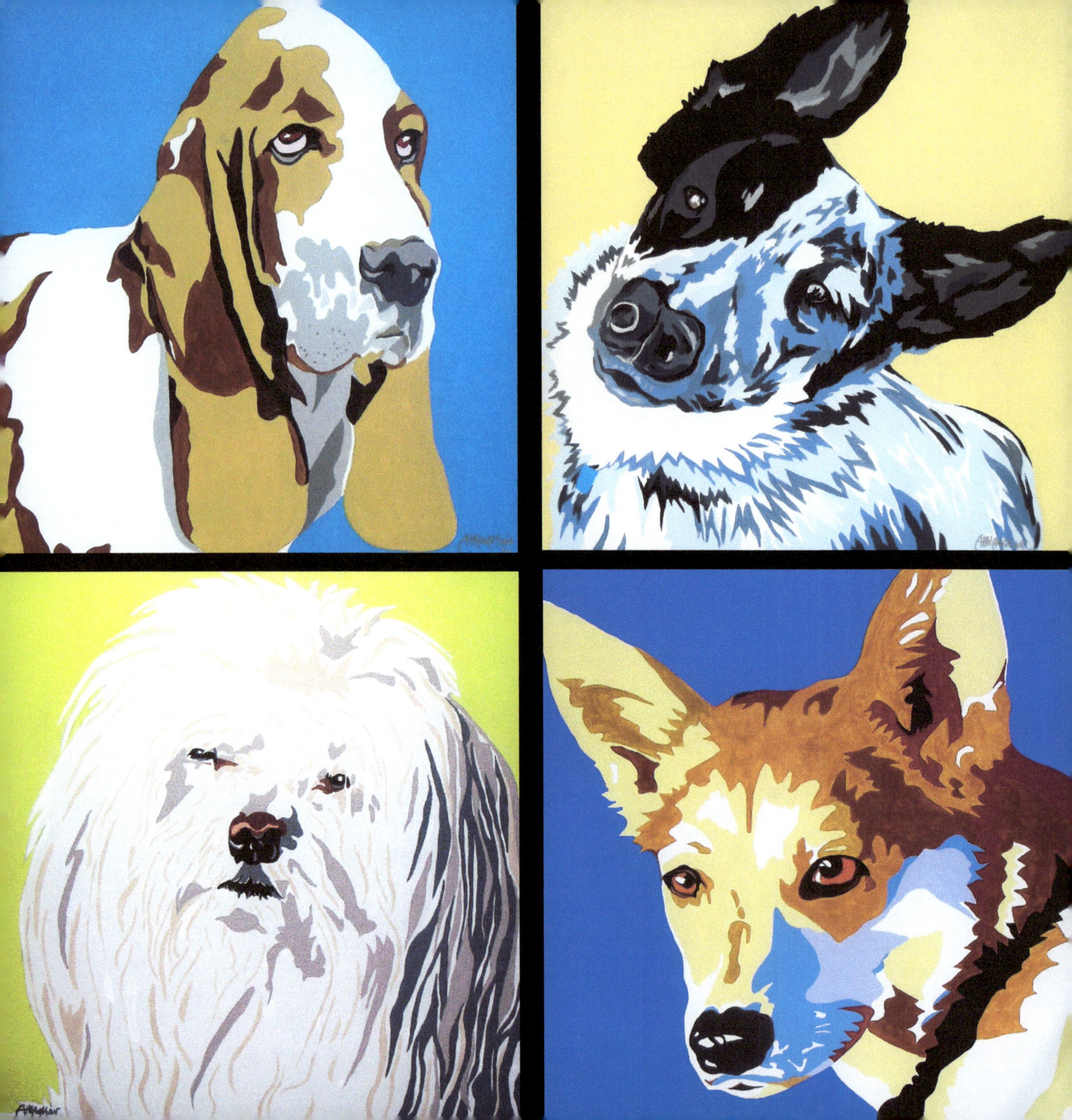

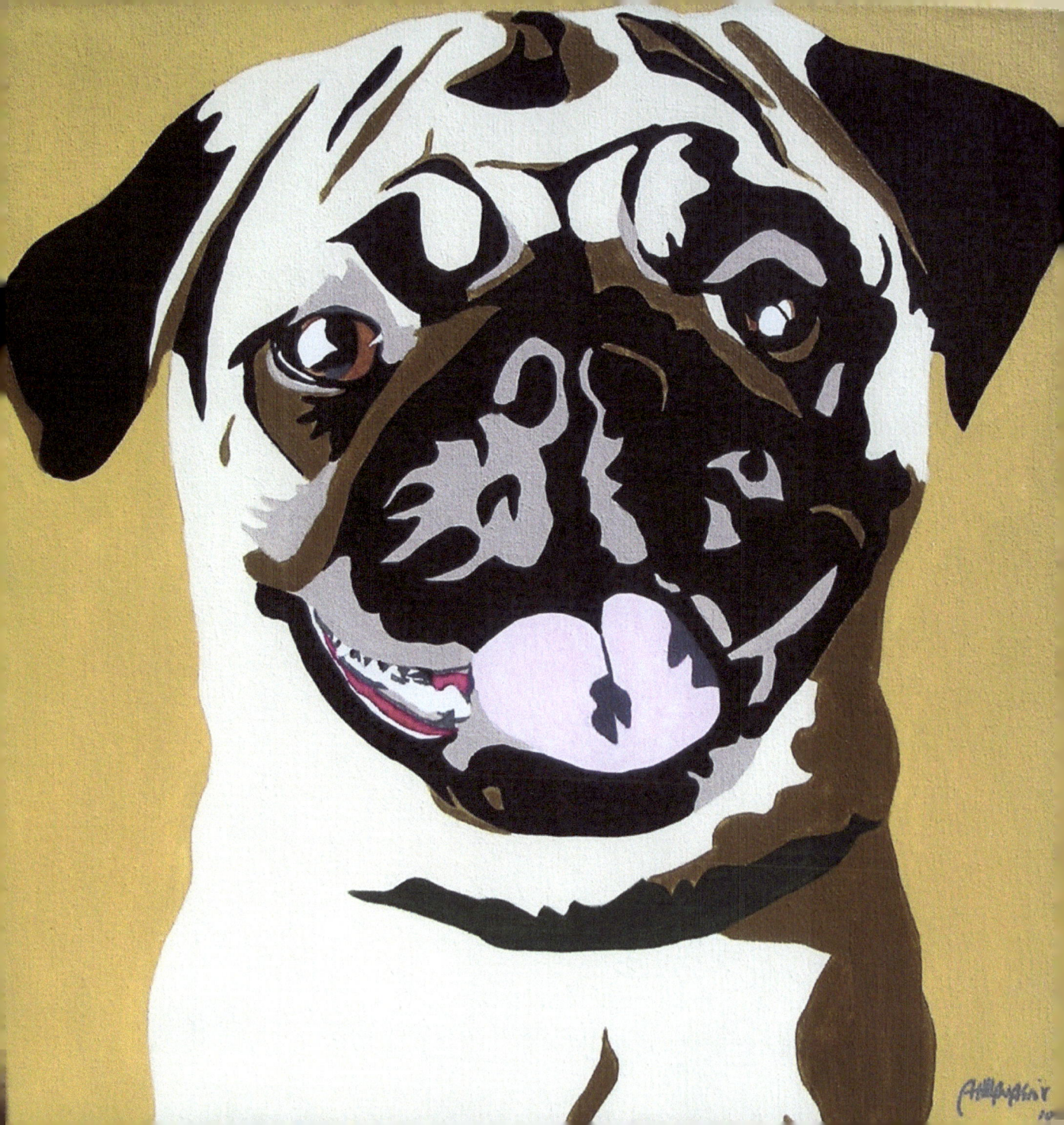

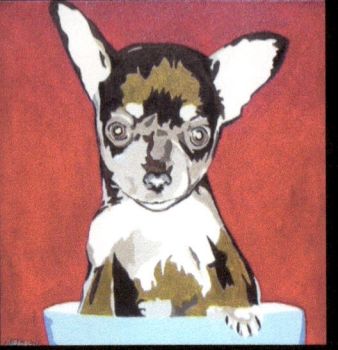
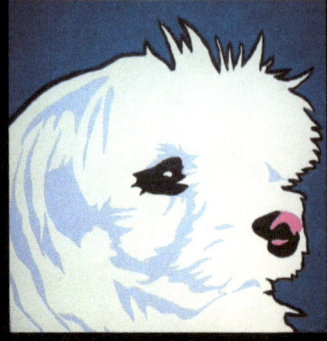
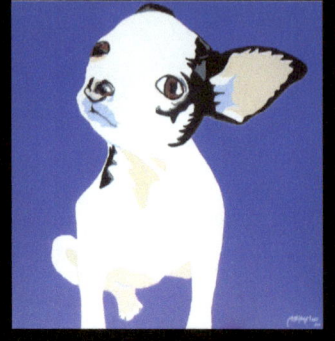

Styles Change: You have 4 years ('09-'12) of paintings on these two pages. Different styles morphing into the more detailed portrait like the one below.

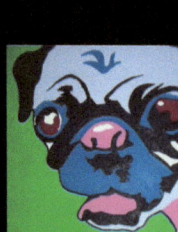

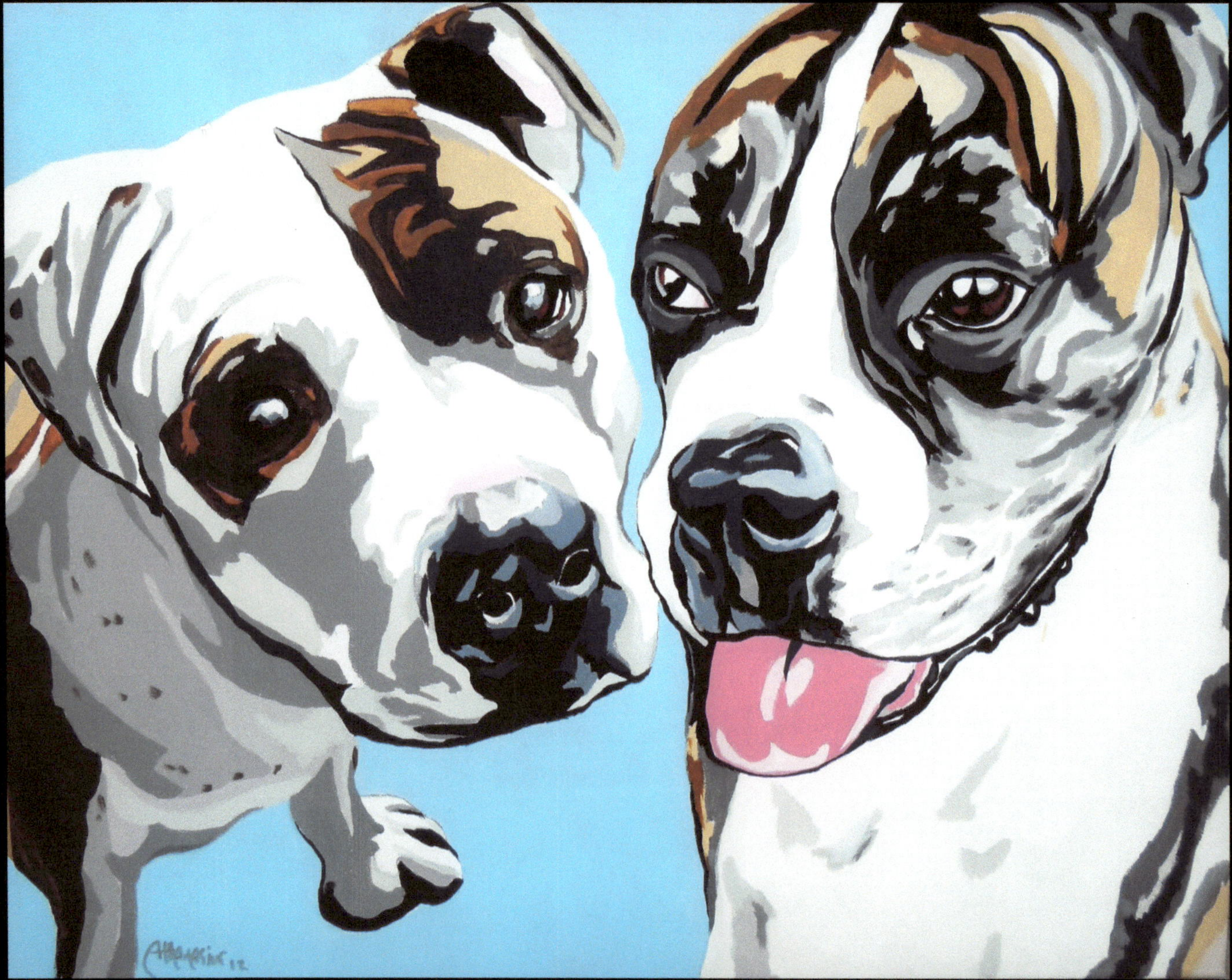

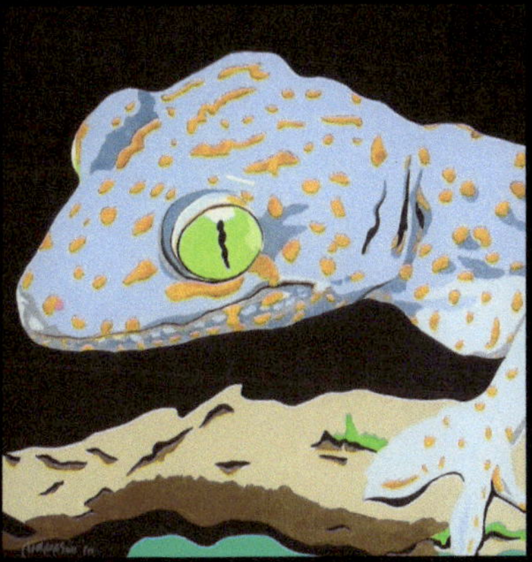

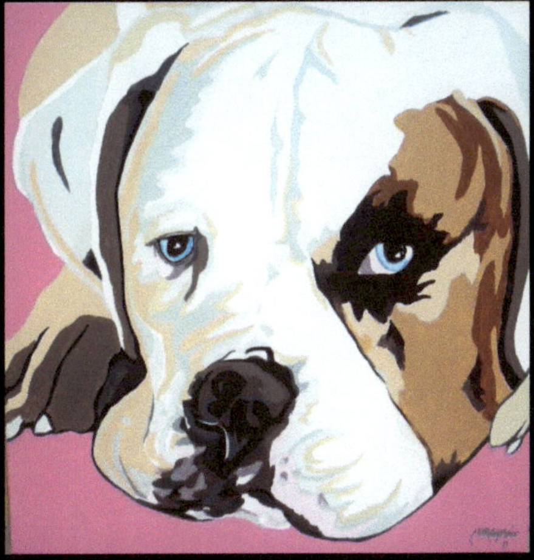

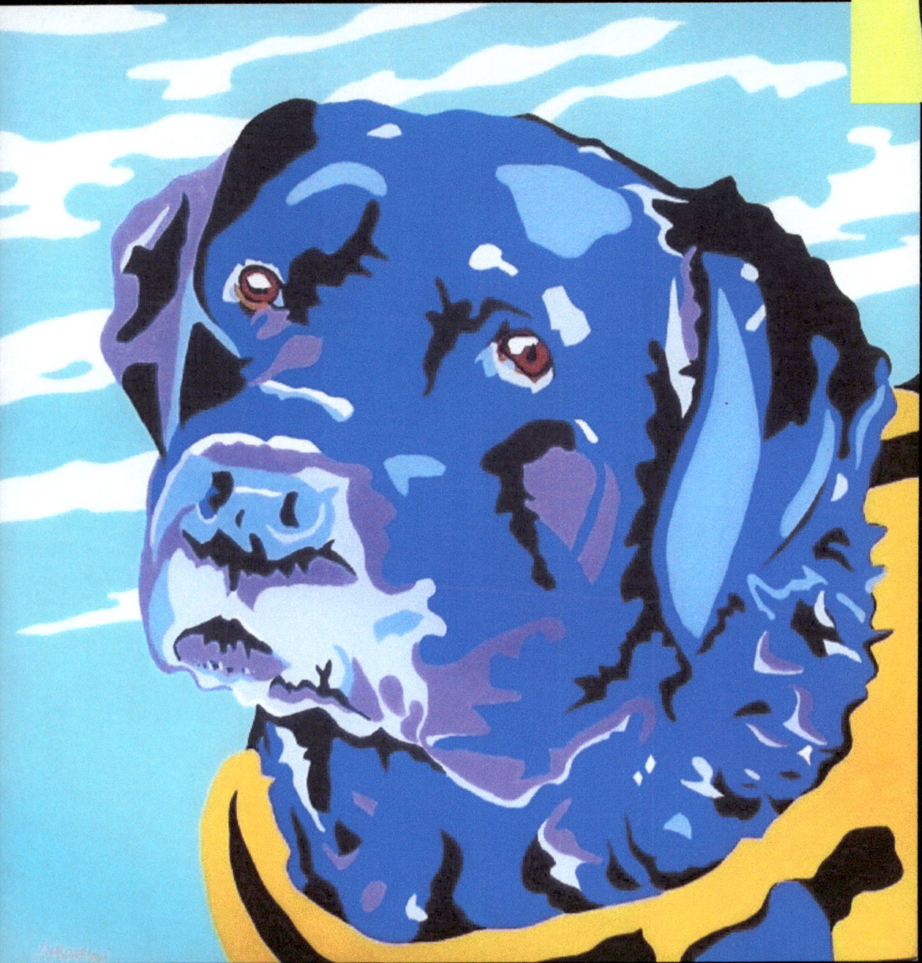

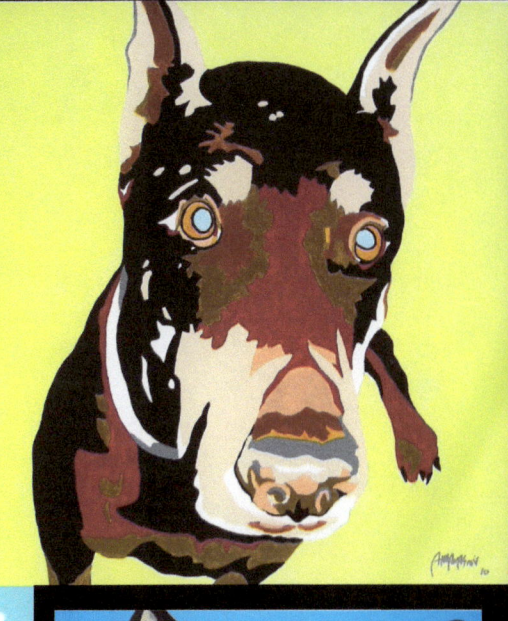
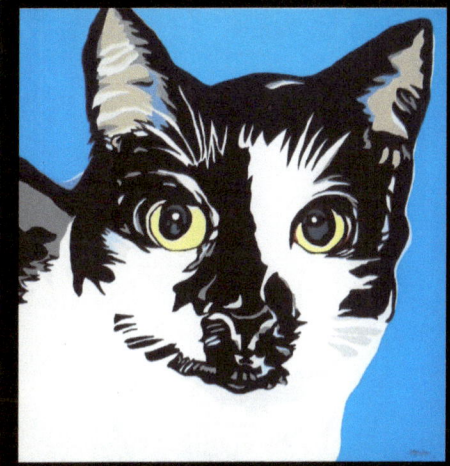
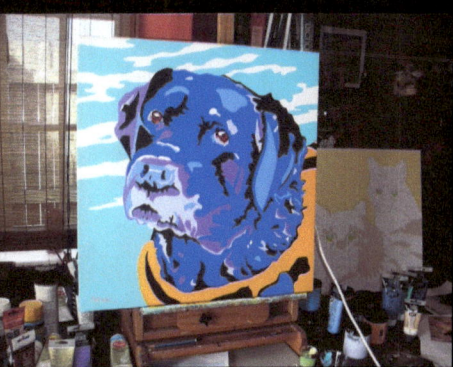

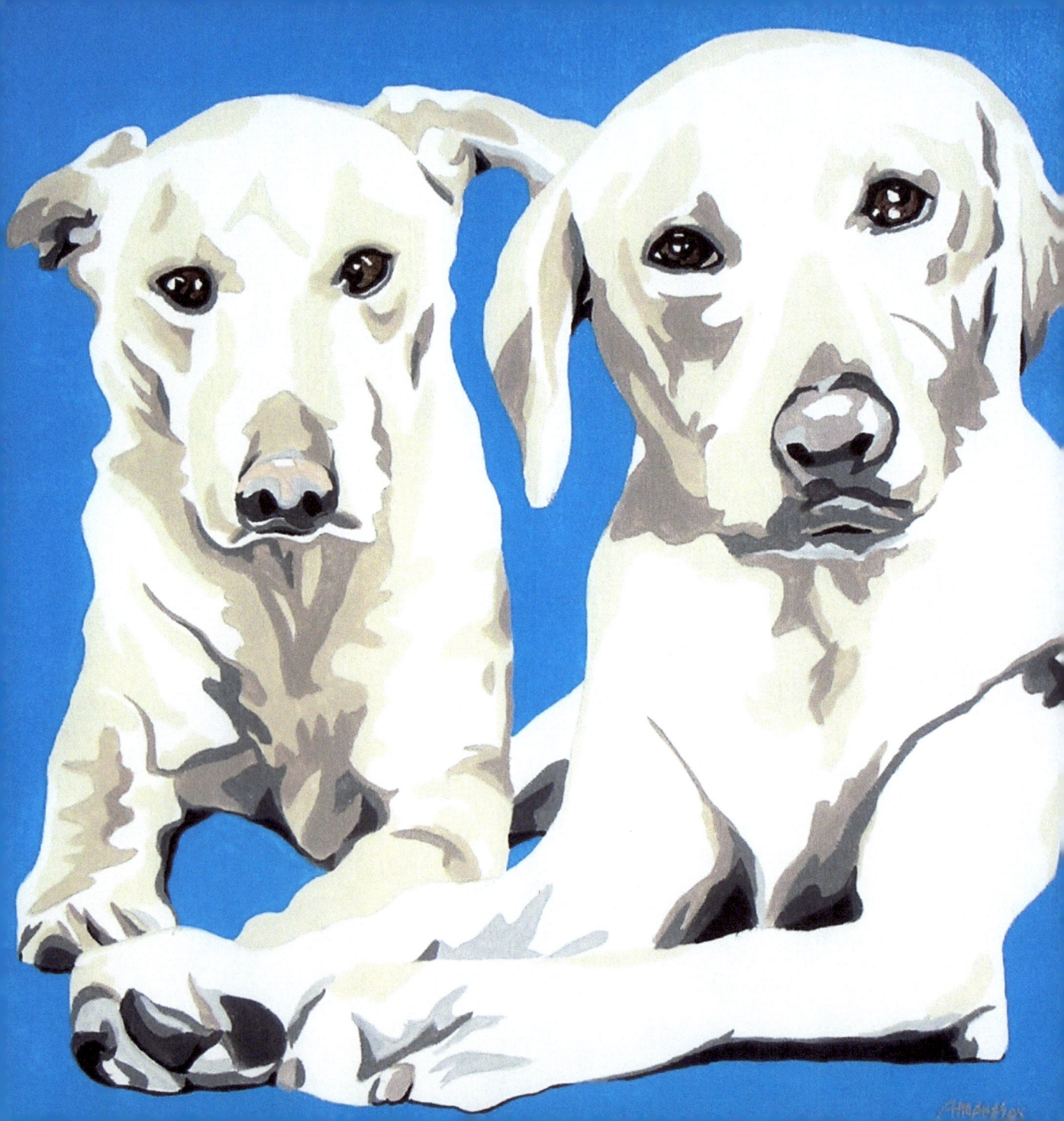

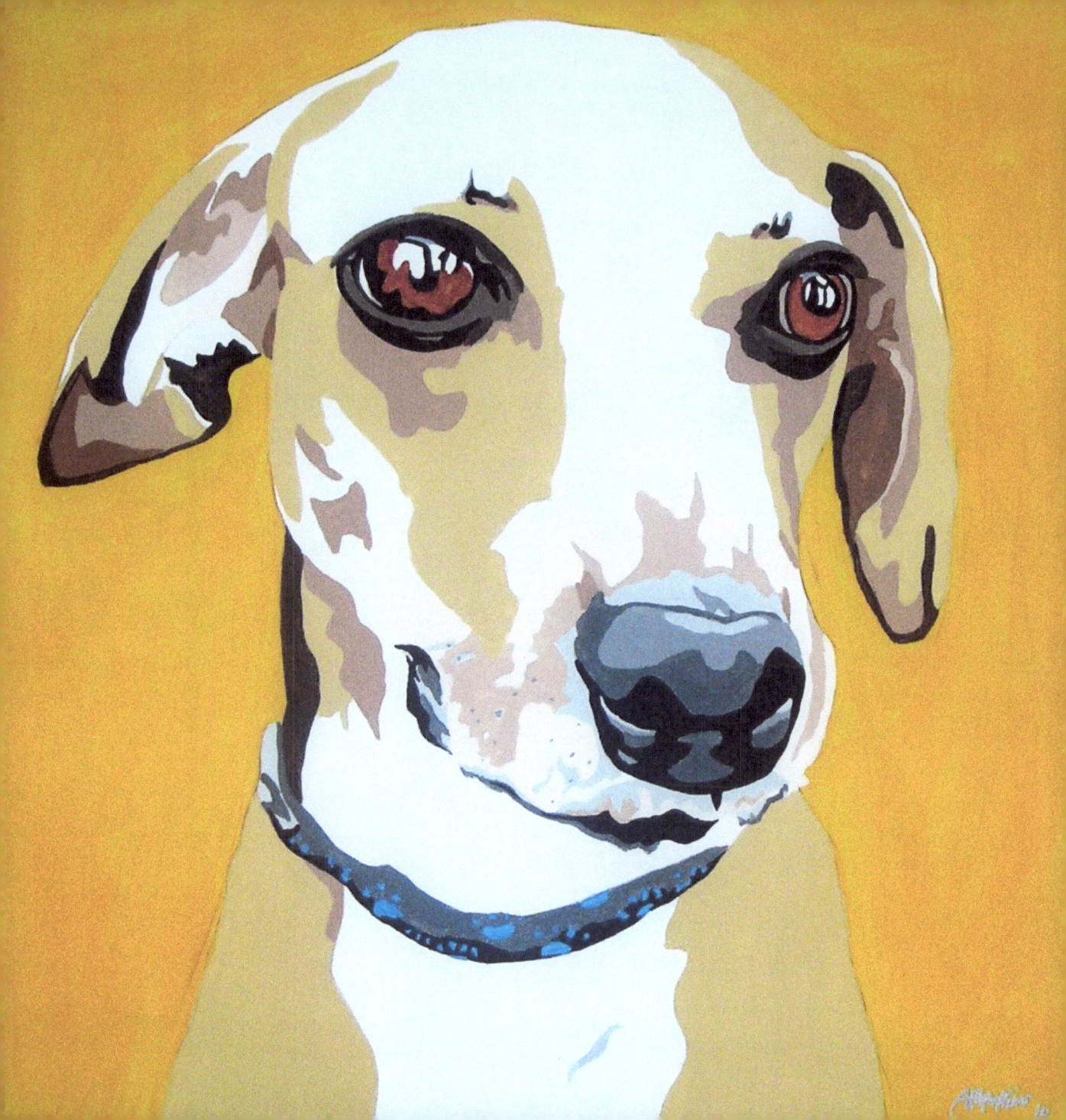

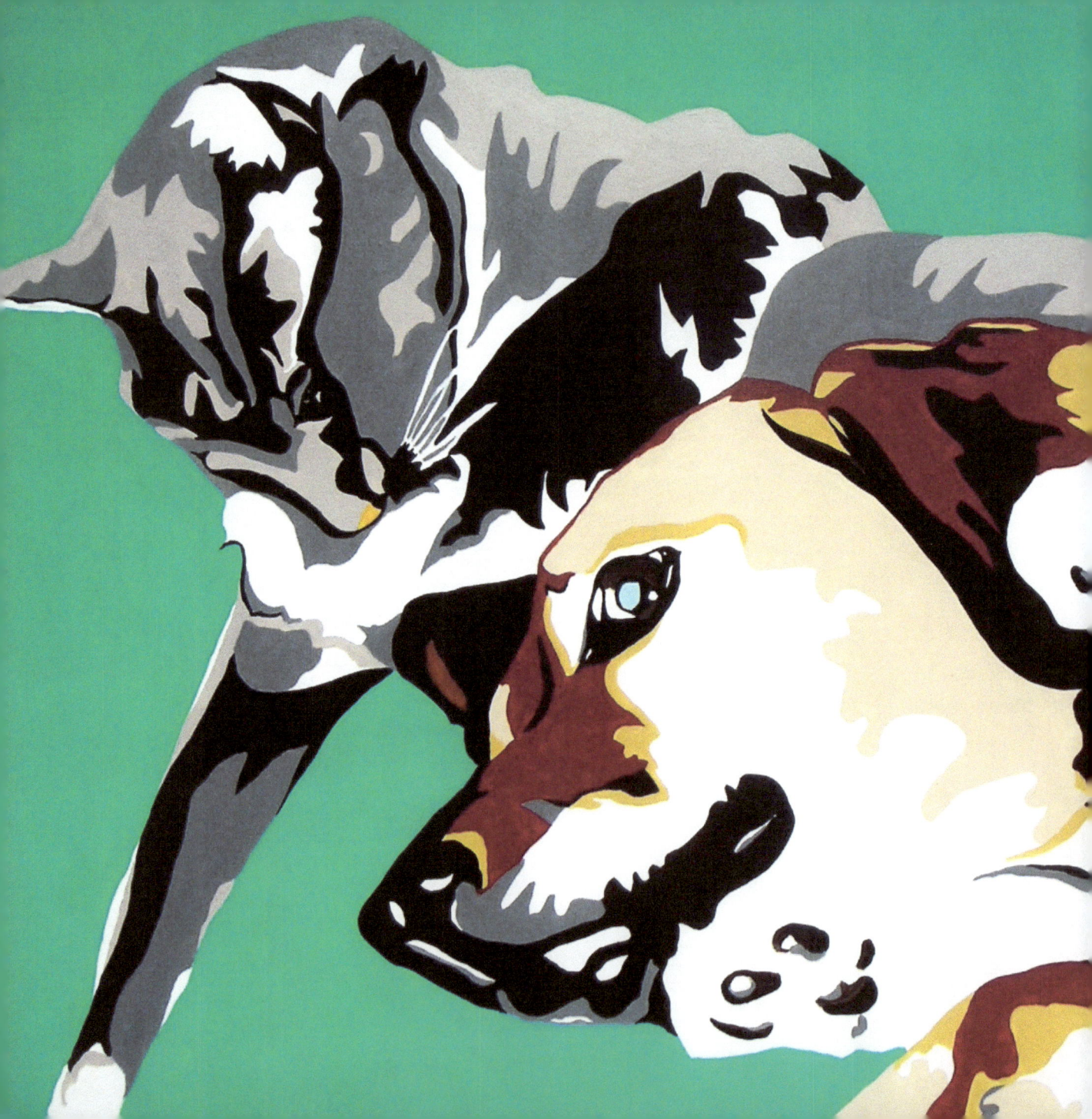

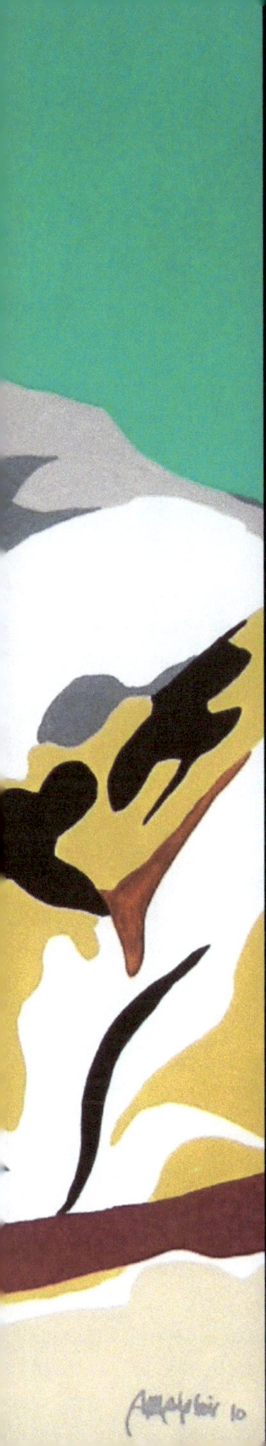

Since we are located in South Florida, I might as well utilize nature in the drying process. Especially the big ones like the to the right.

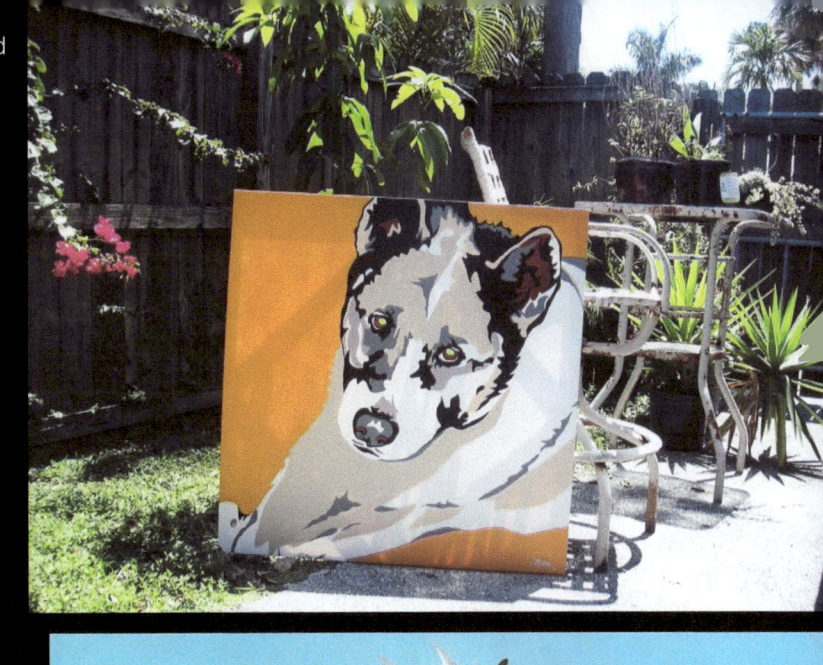

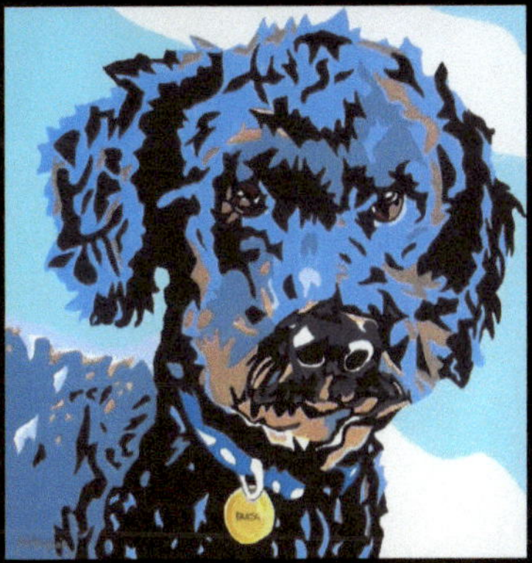

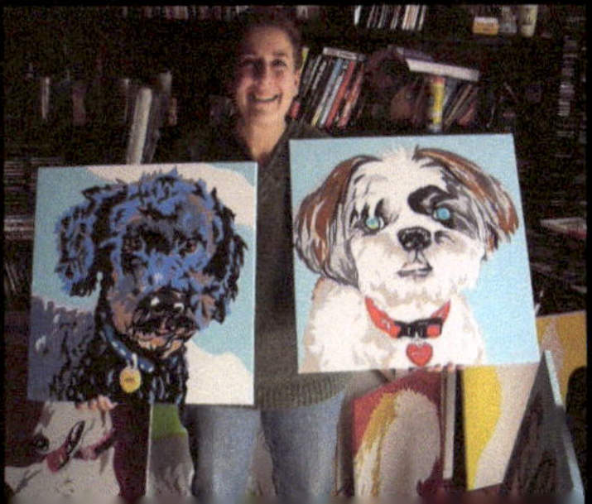

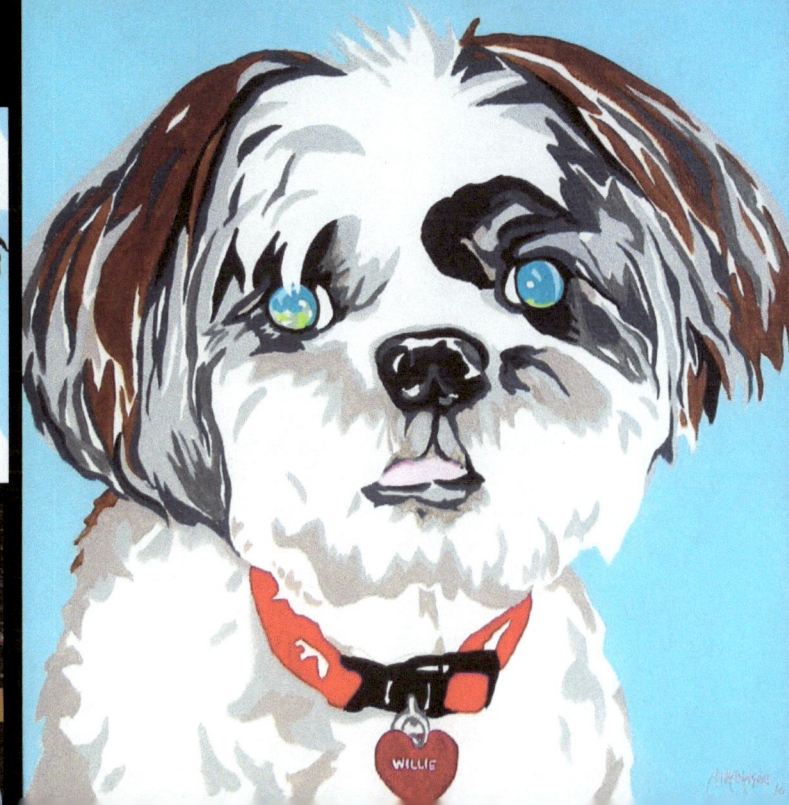

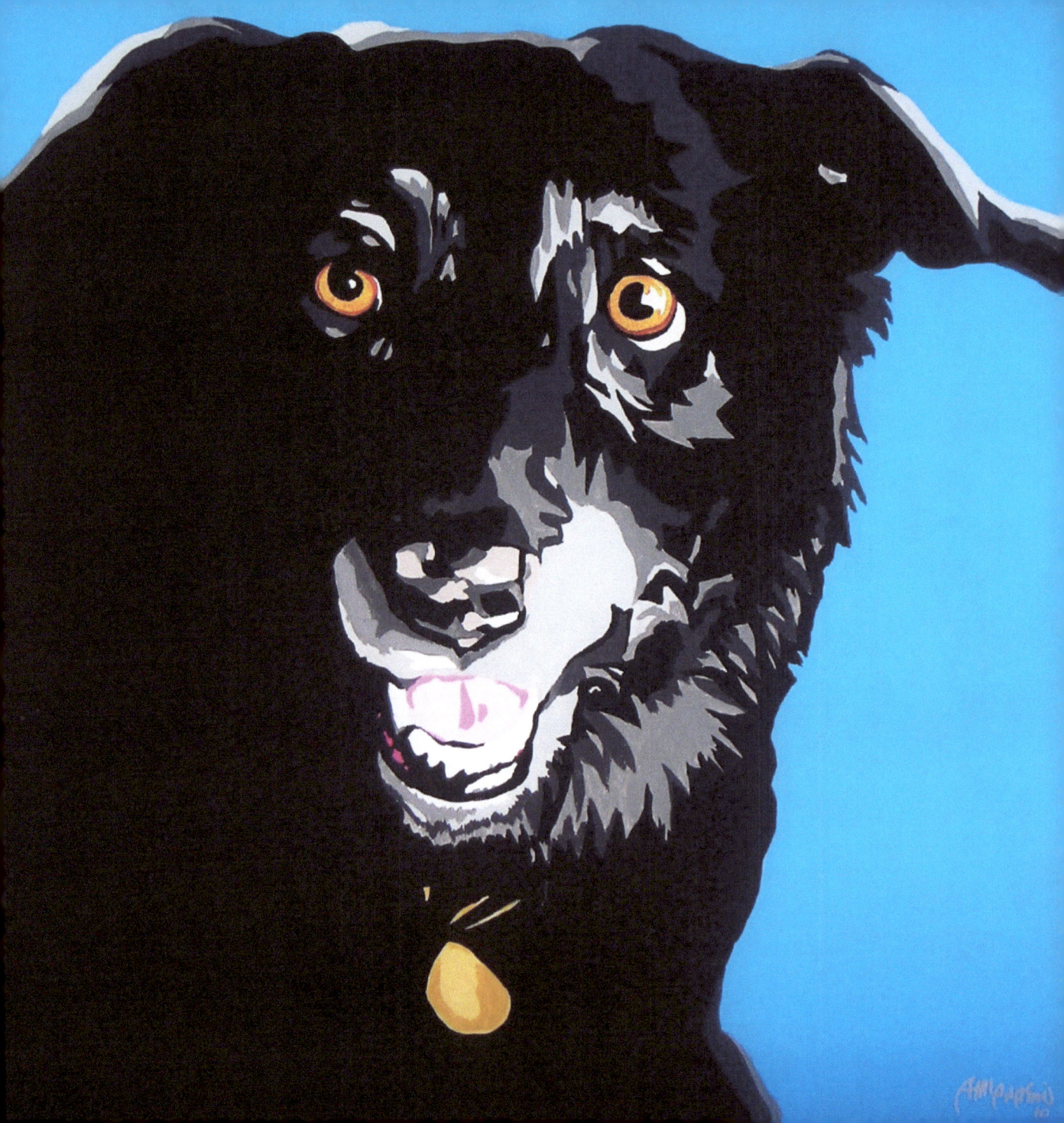

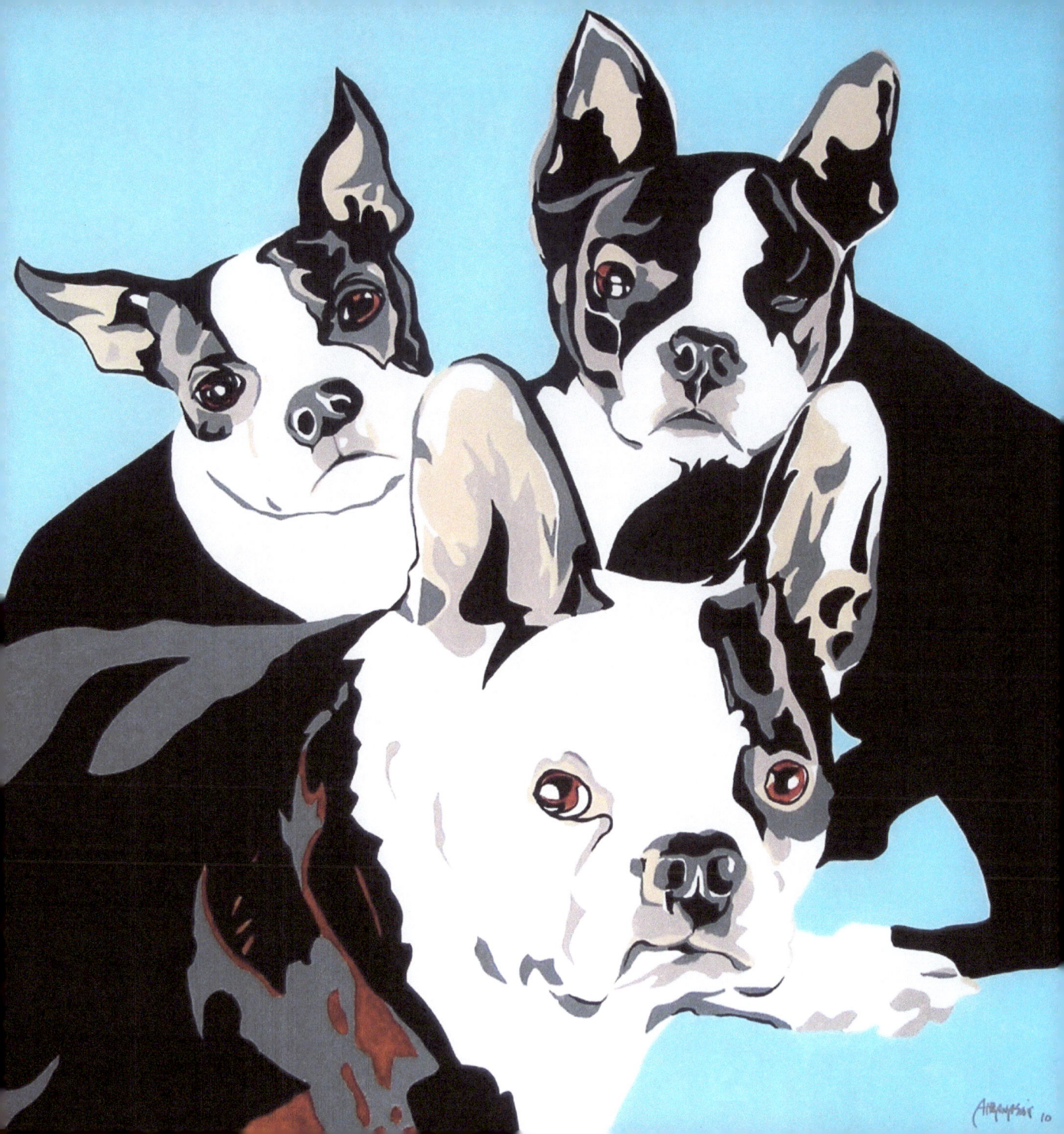

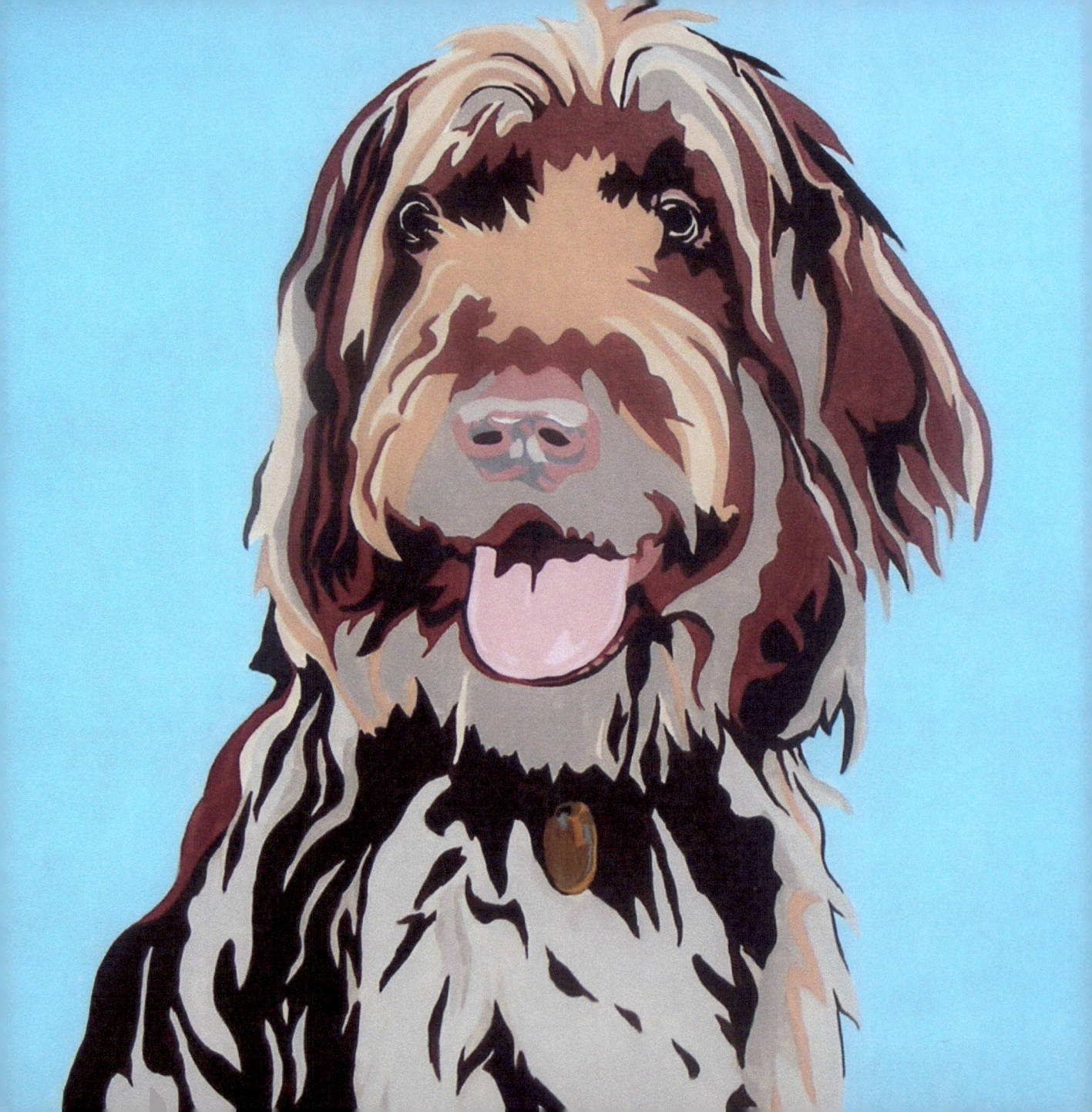

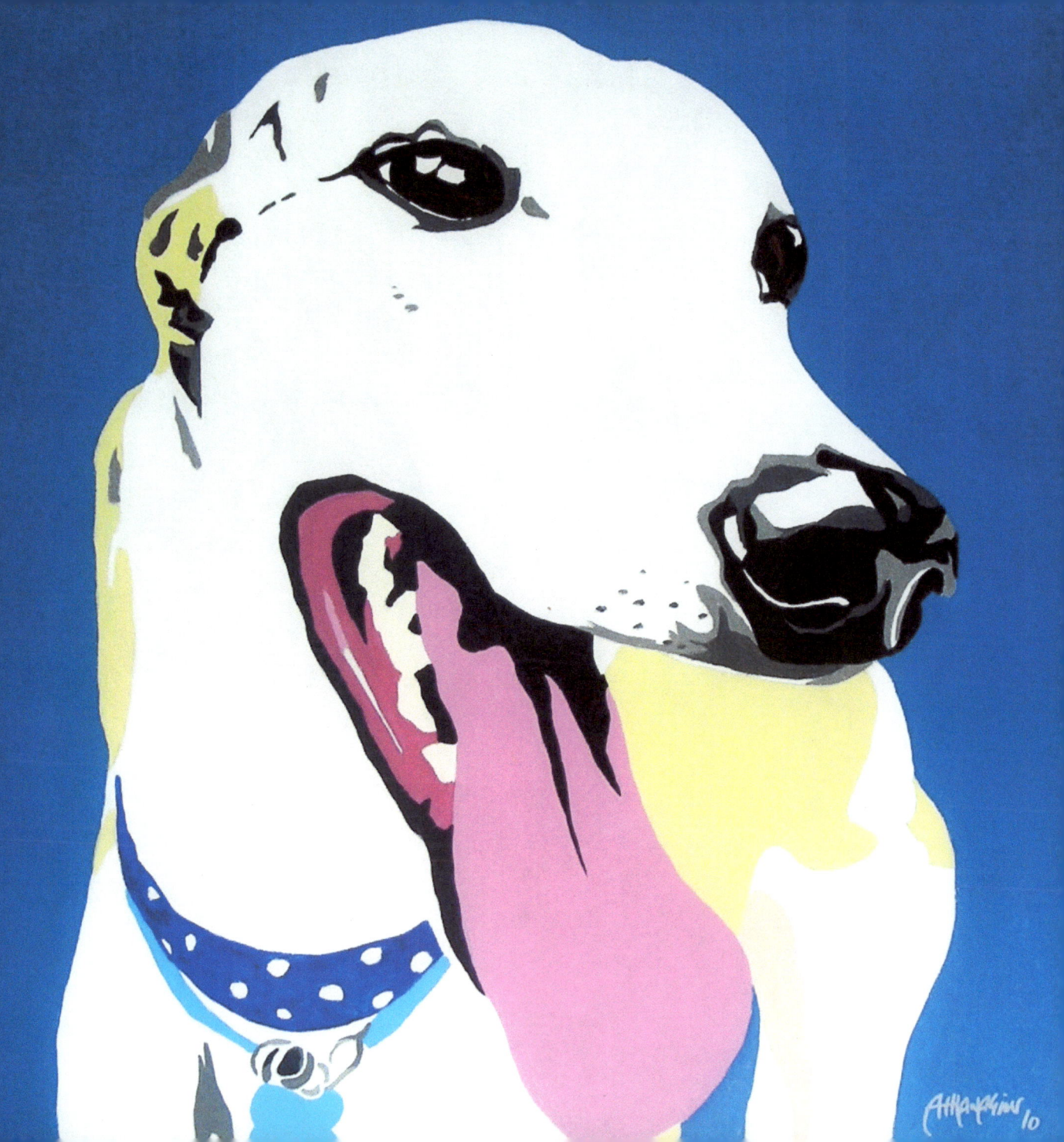

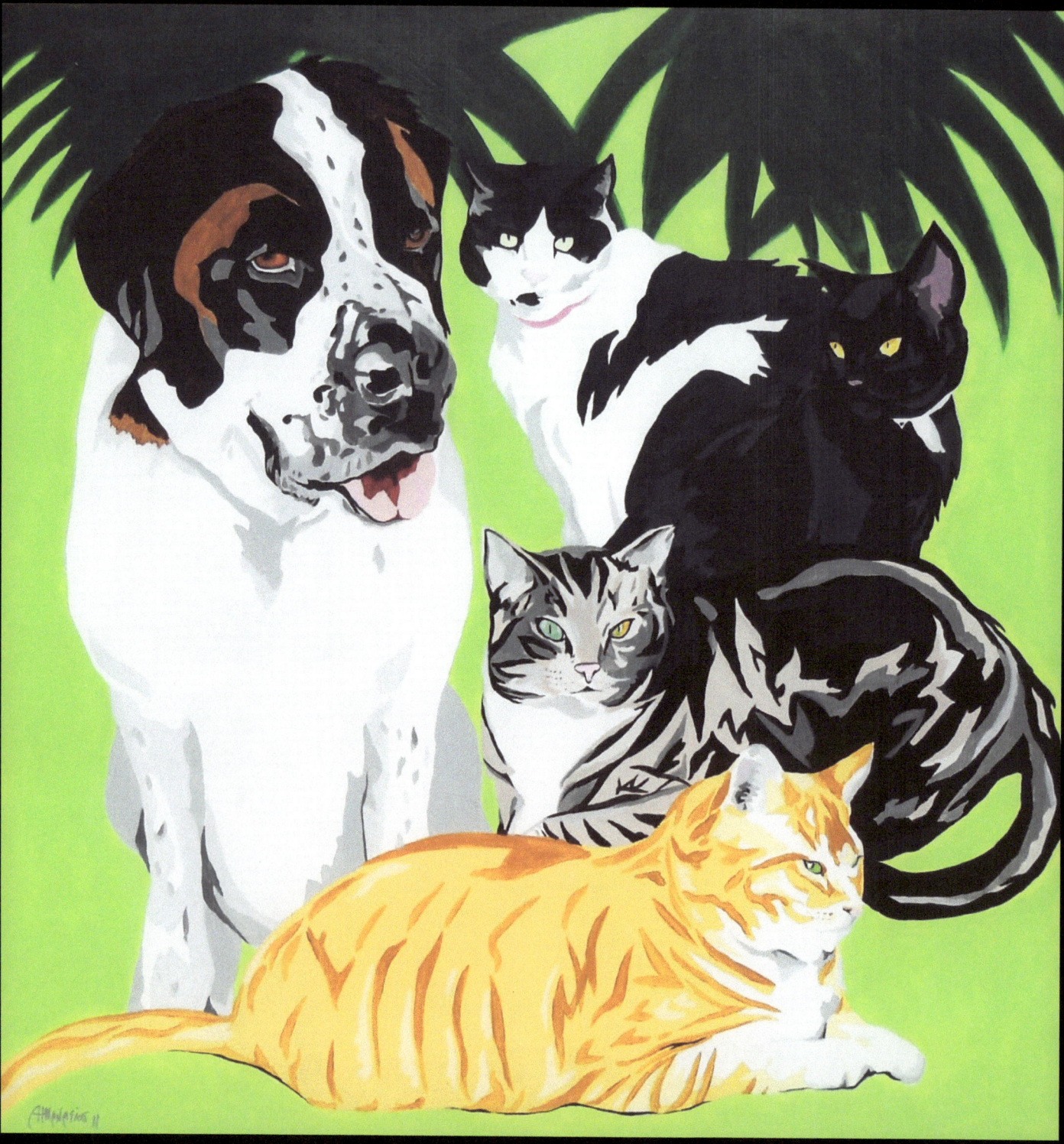

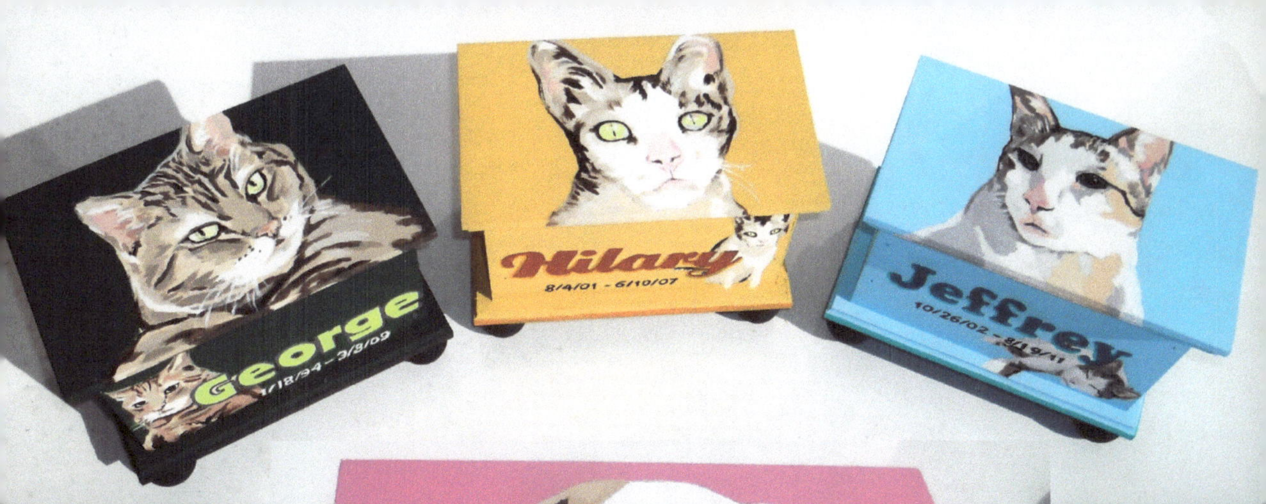

George
7/18/94 - 3/3/09

Hilary
8/4/01 - 6/10/07

Jeffrey
10/26/02 - 3/19/11

Devoted Love
Forever: Pop Pet
Urns, which feature
two portraits per
wooden urn.

Millie
9/25/98 - 1/9/11

Louie
7/10/97 - 1/22/11

Millie
9/25/98 - 1/9/11

Cooper
3/1/10 - 6/11/11

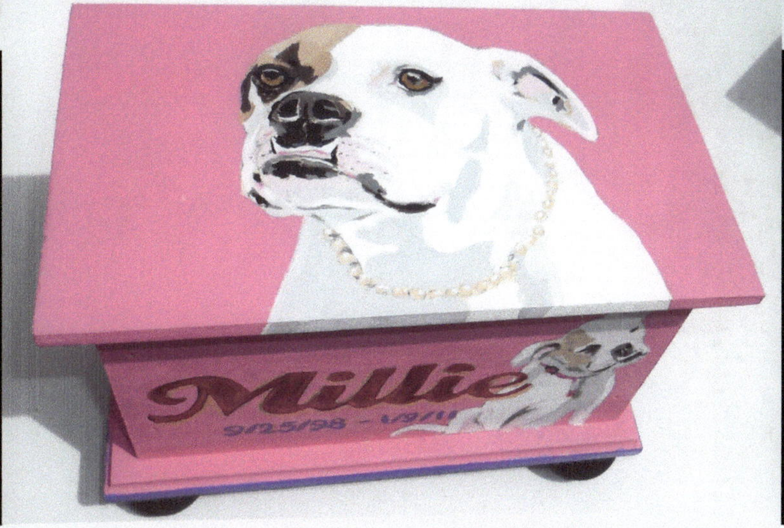

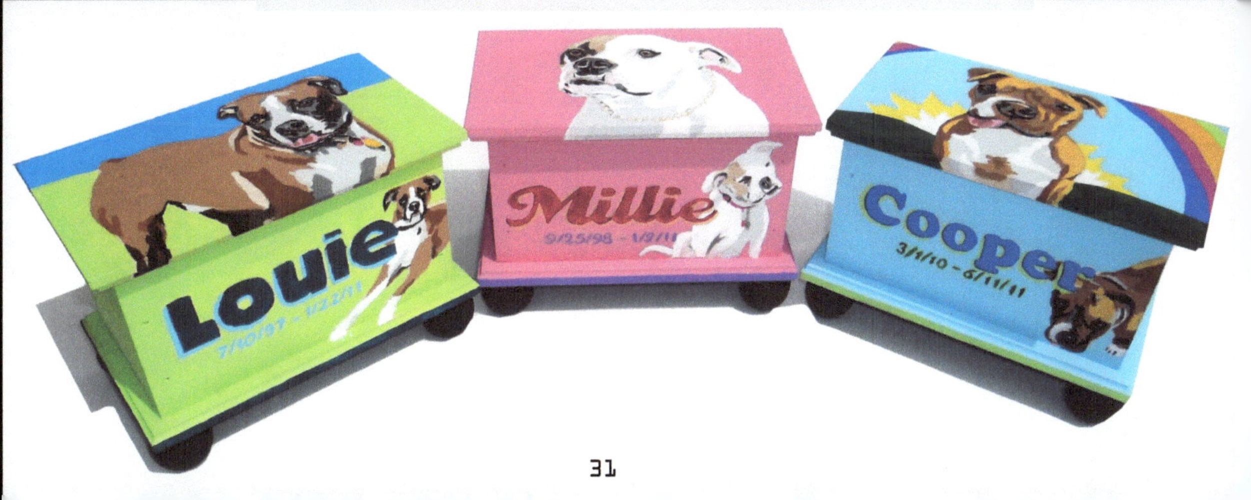

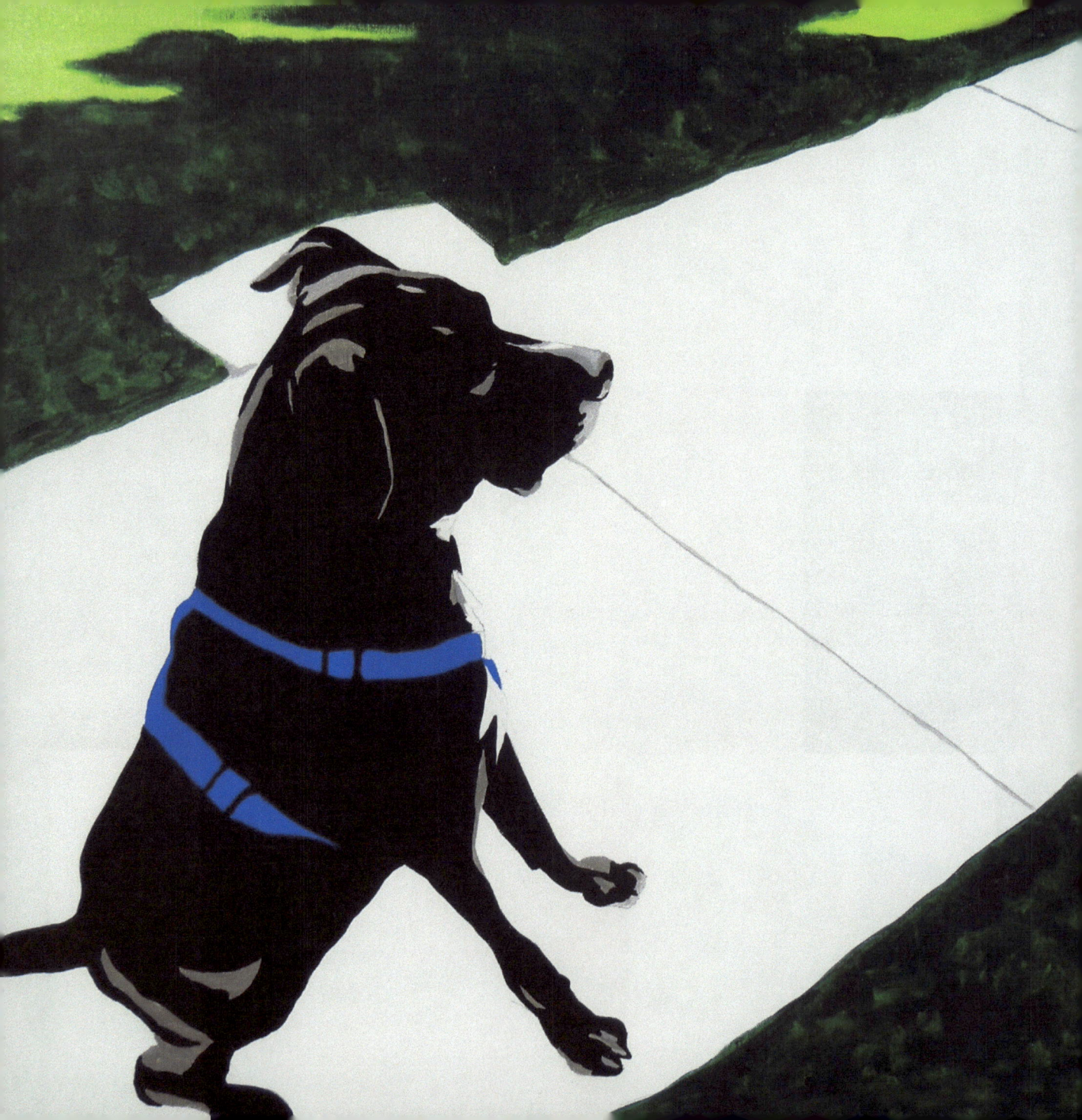

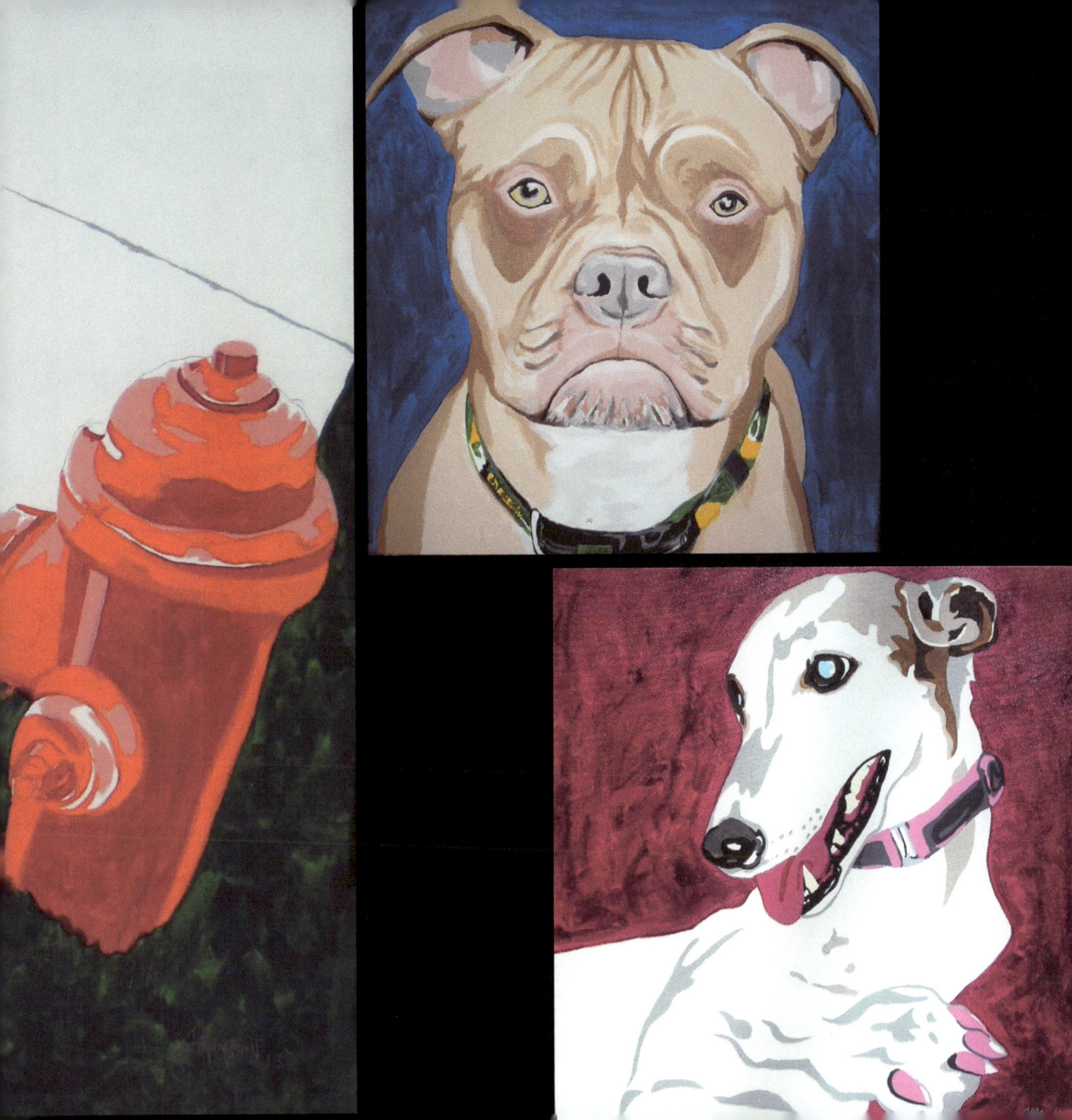

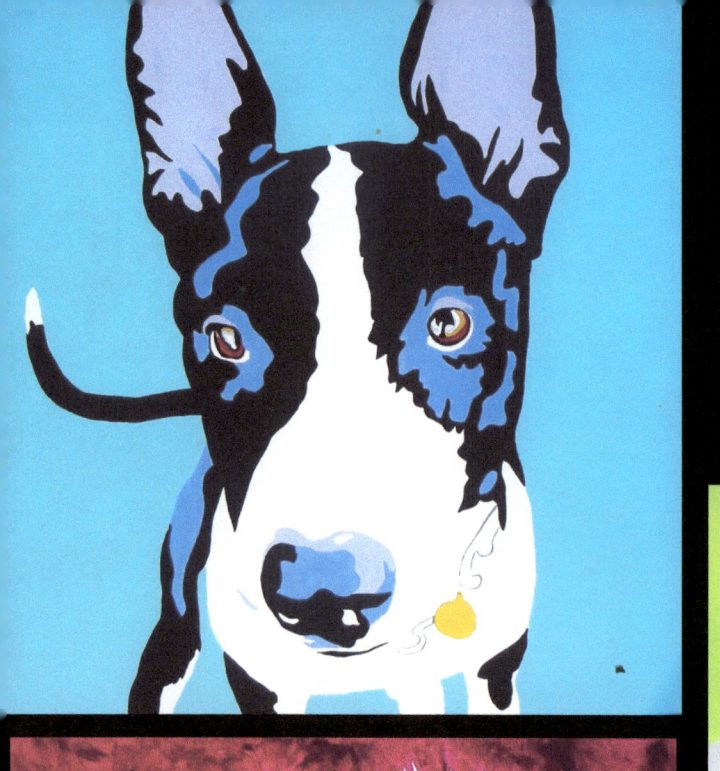

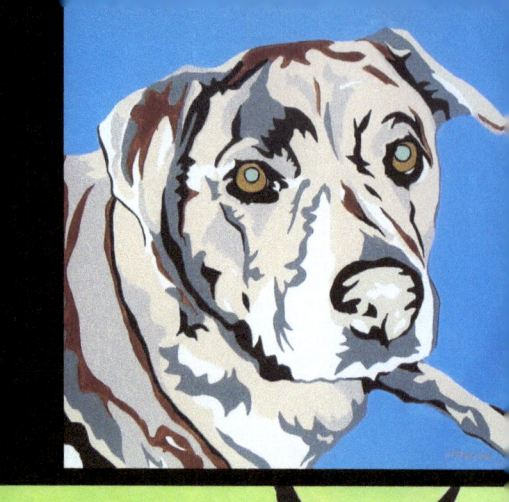

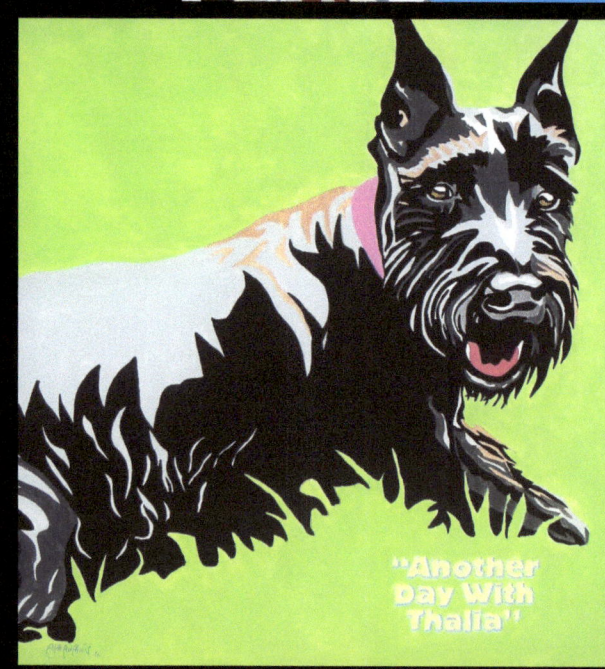

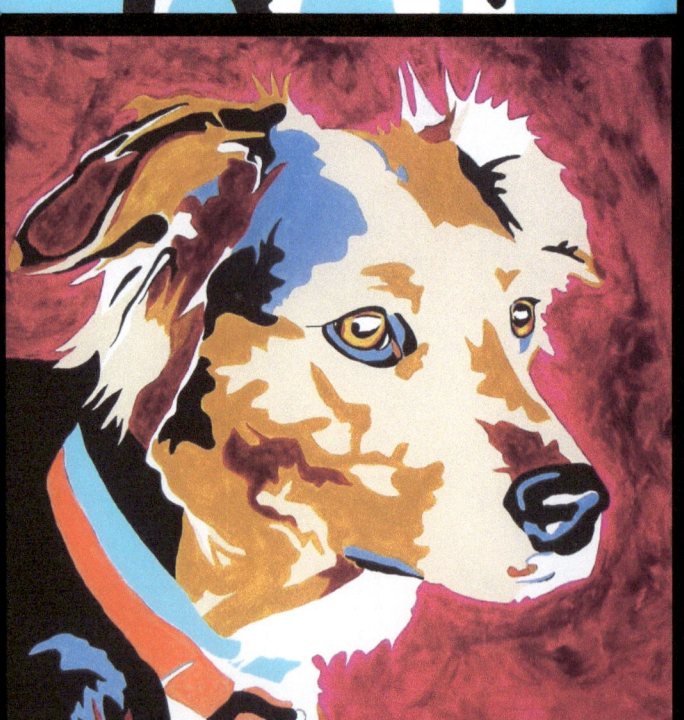

"Another Day With Thalia"

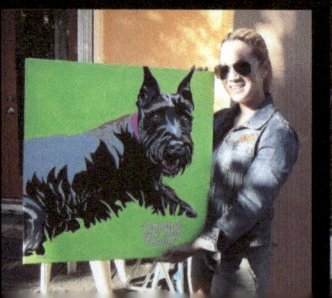

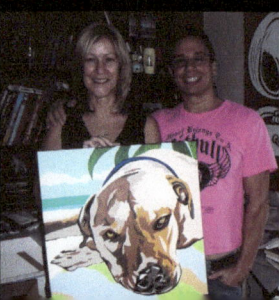

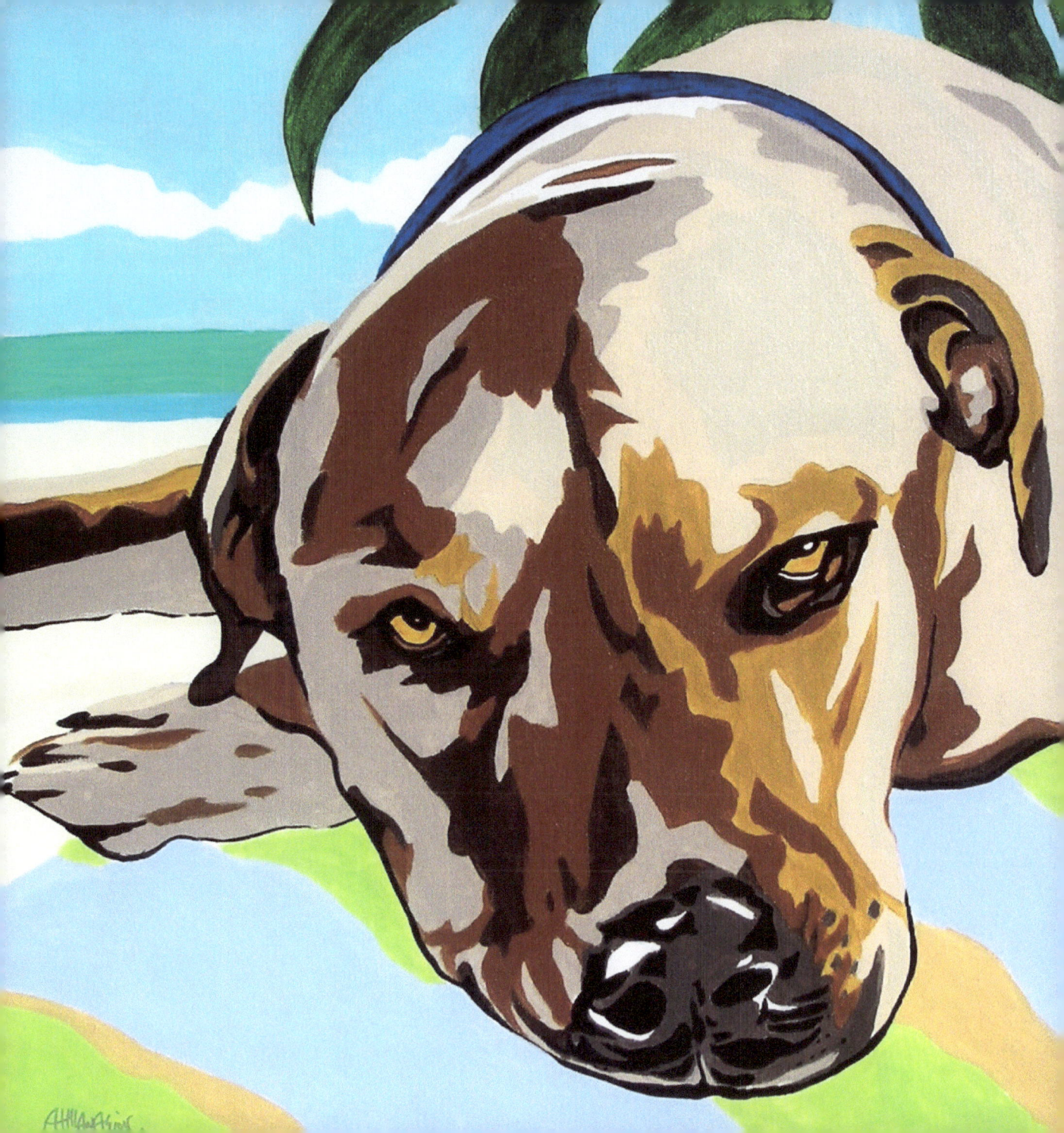

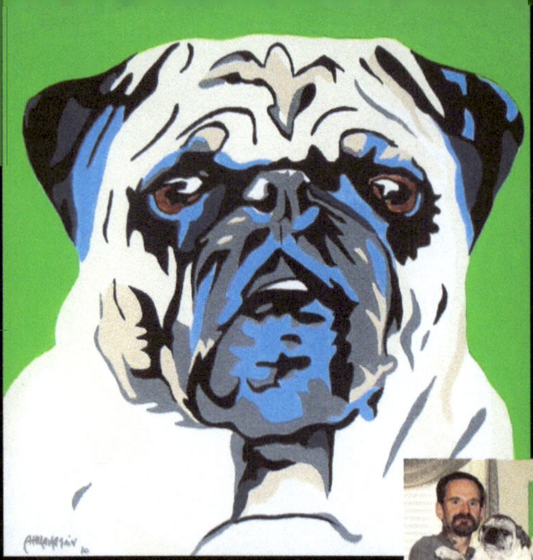

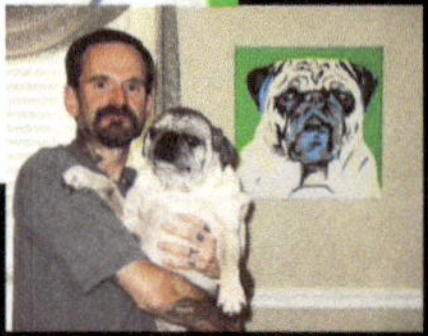

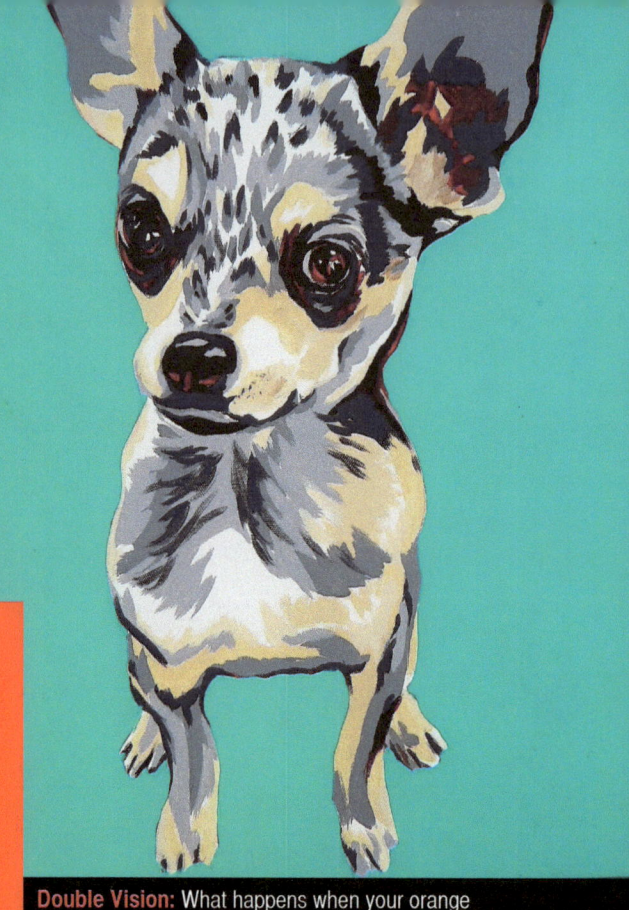

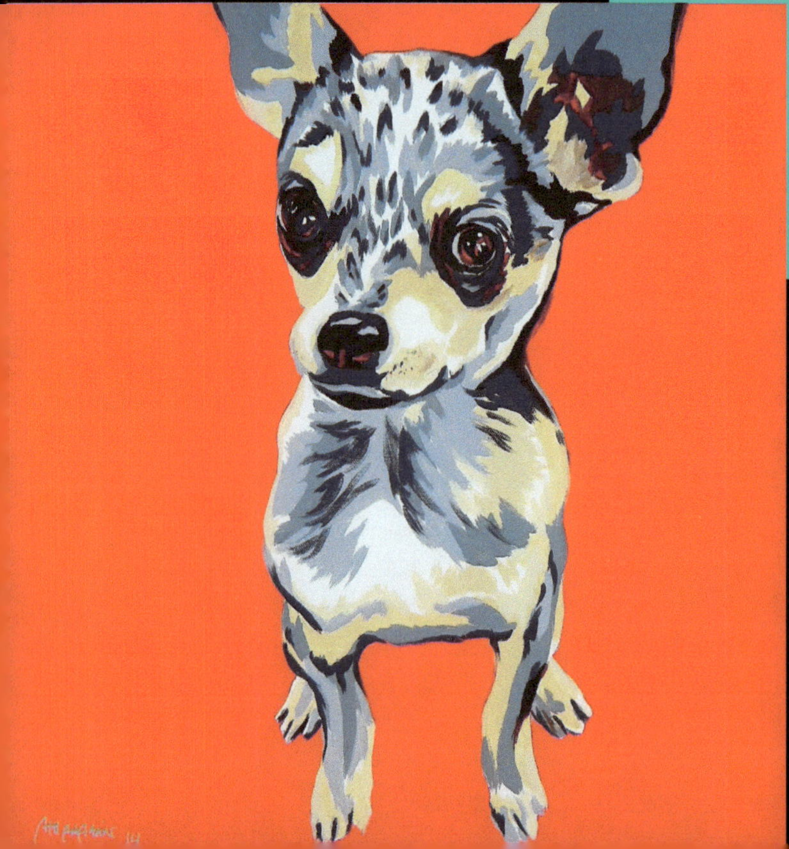

Double Vision: What happens when your orange background doesn't work for the client? You change it. Which one do you like?

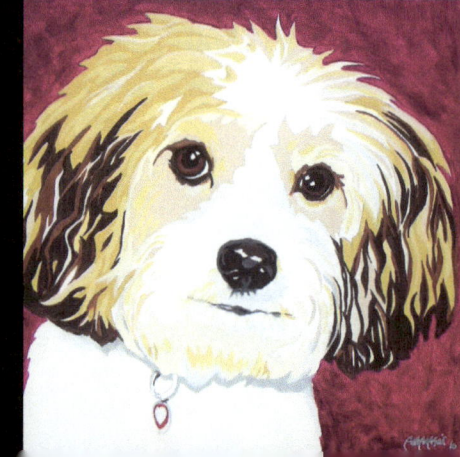

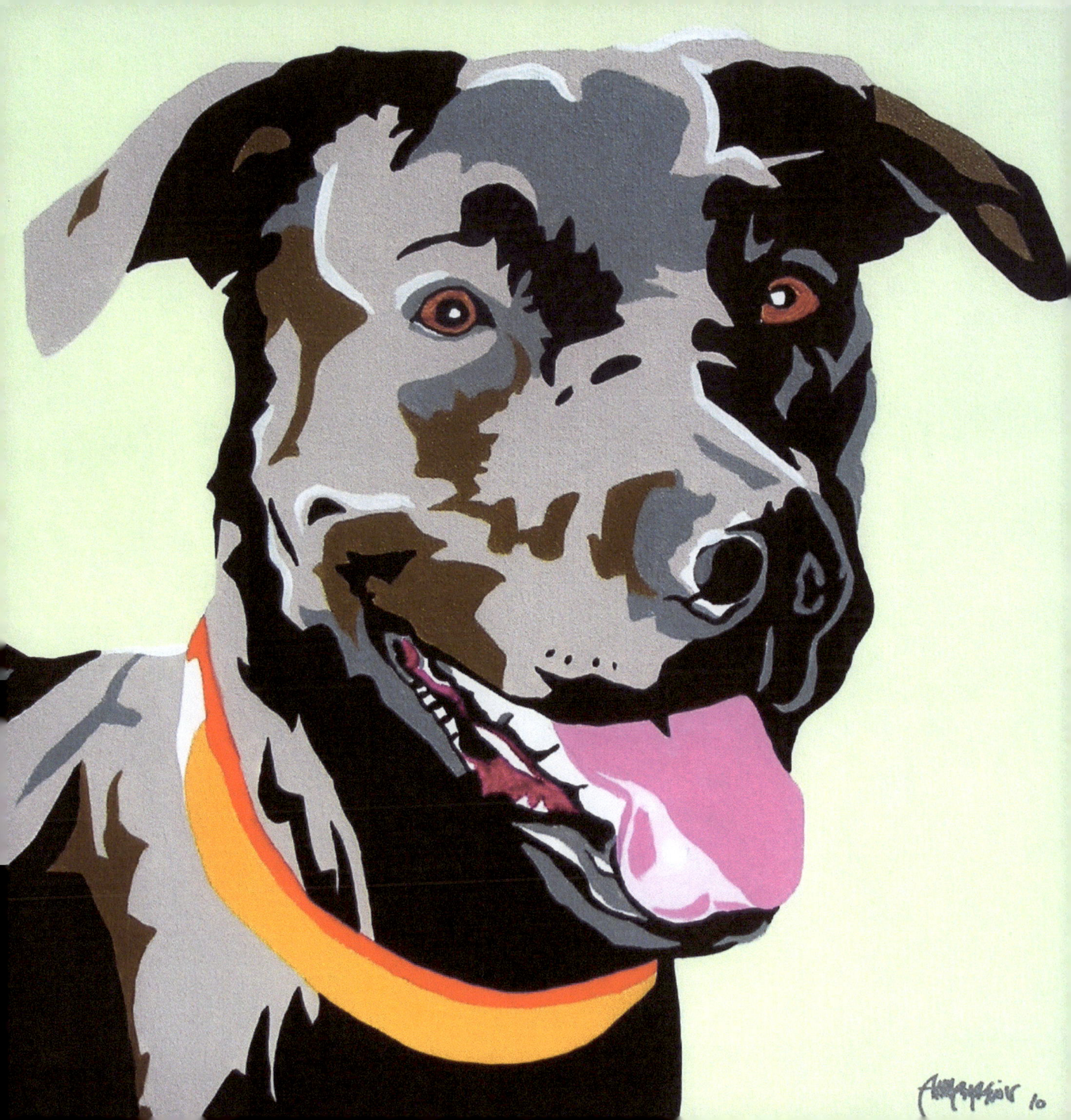

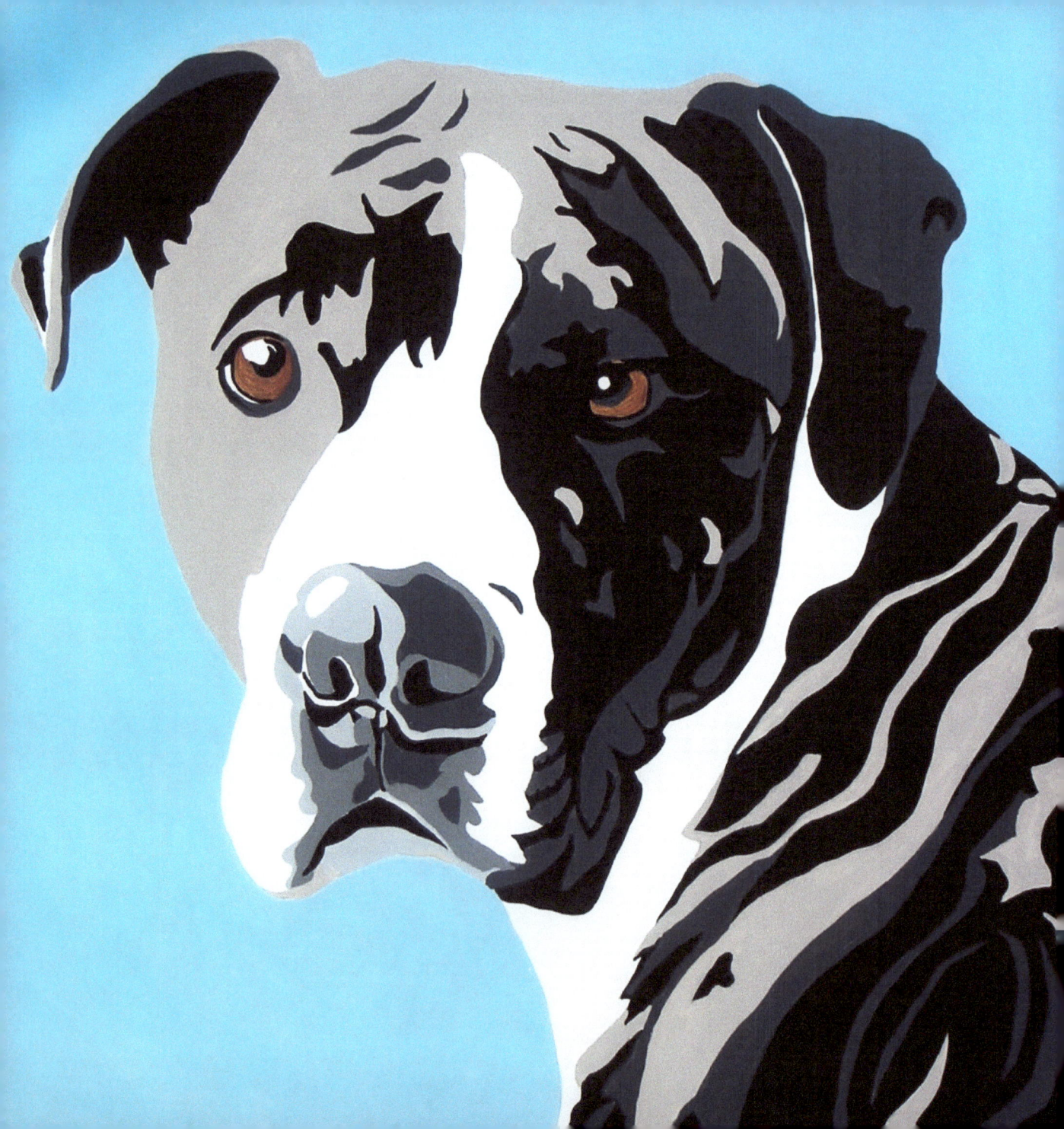

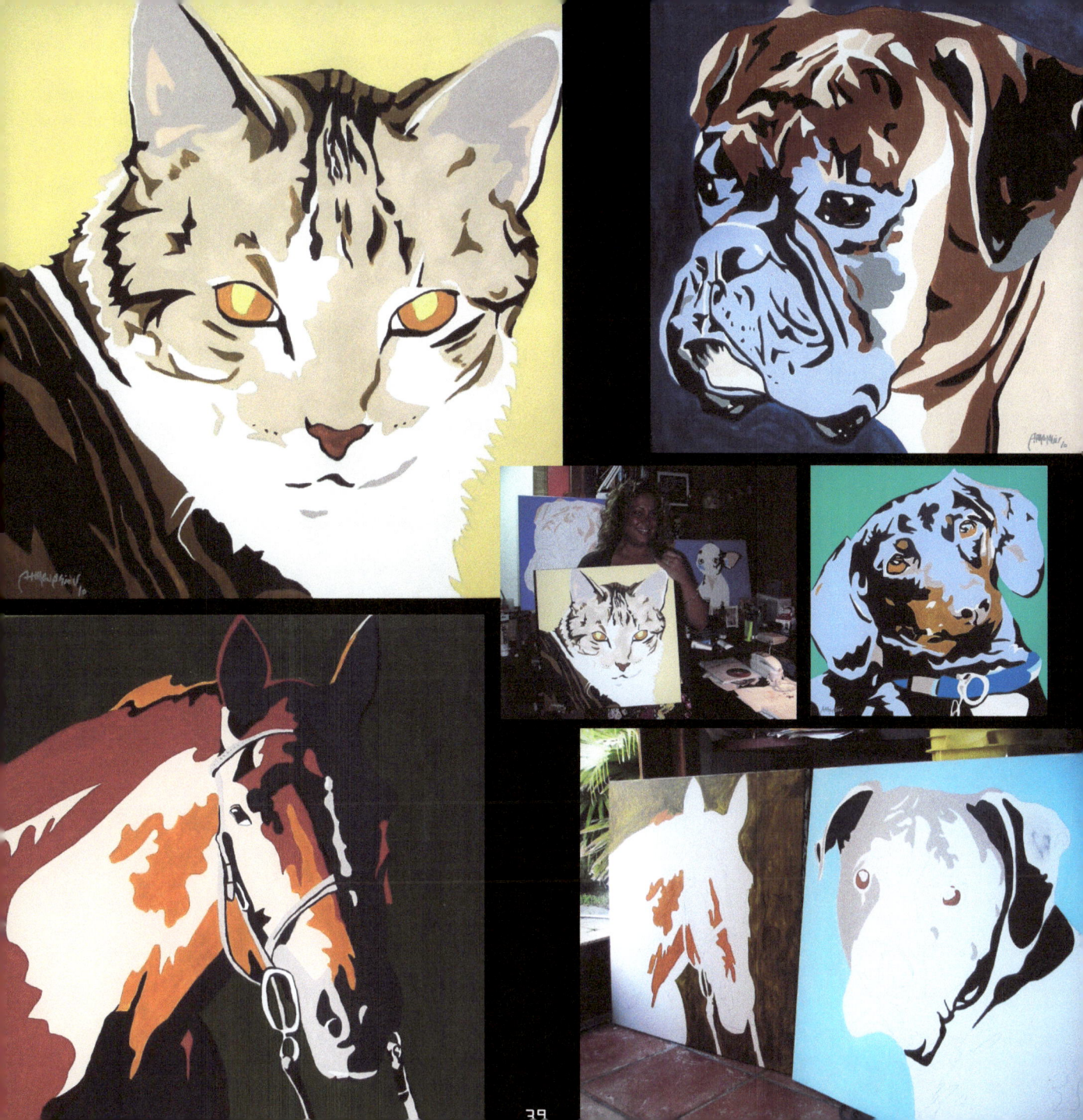

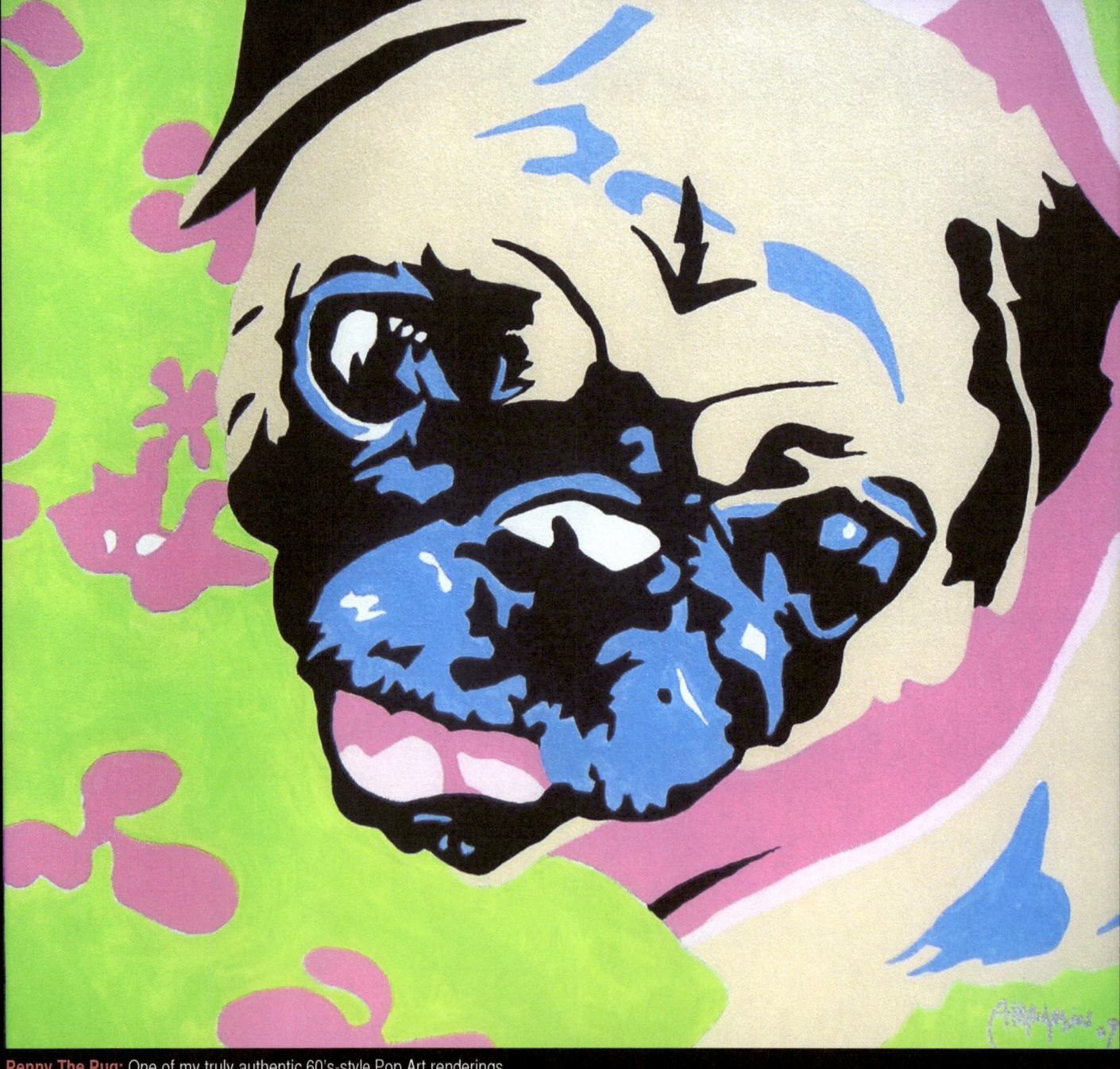

Penny The Pug: One of my truly authentic 60's-style Pop Art renderings.

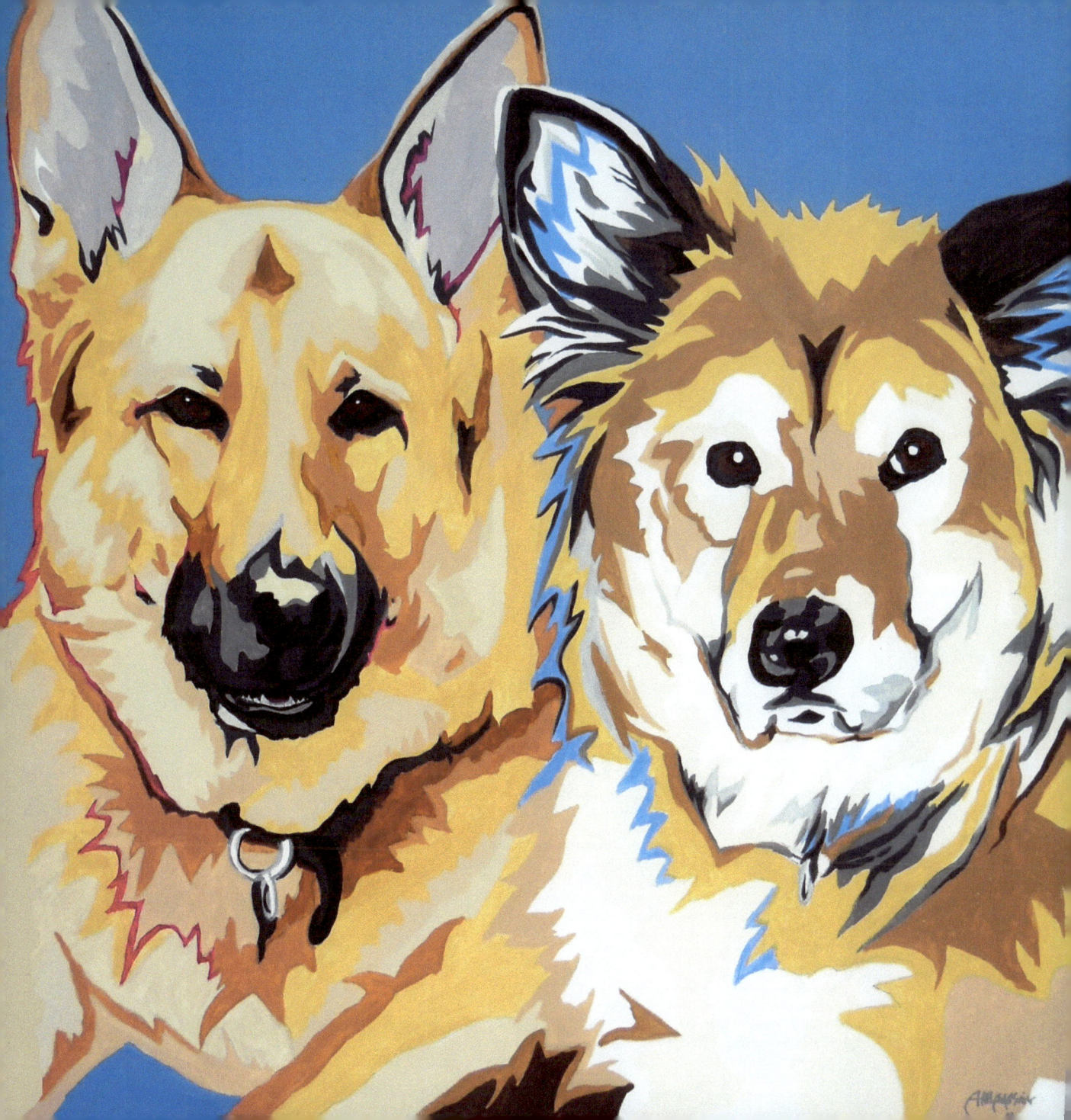

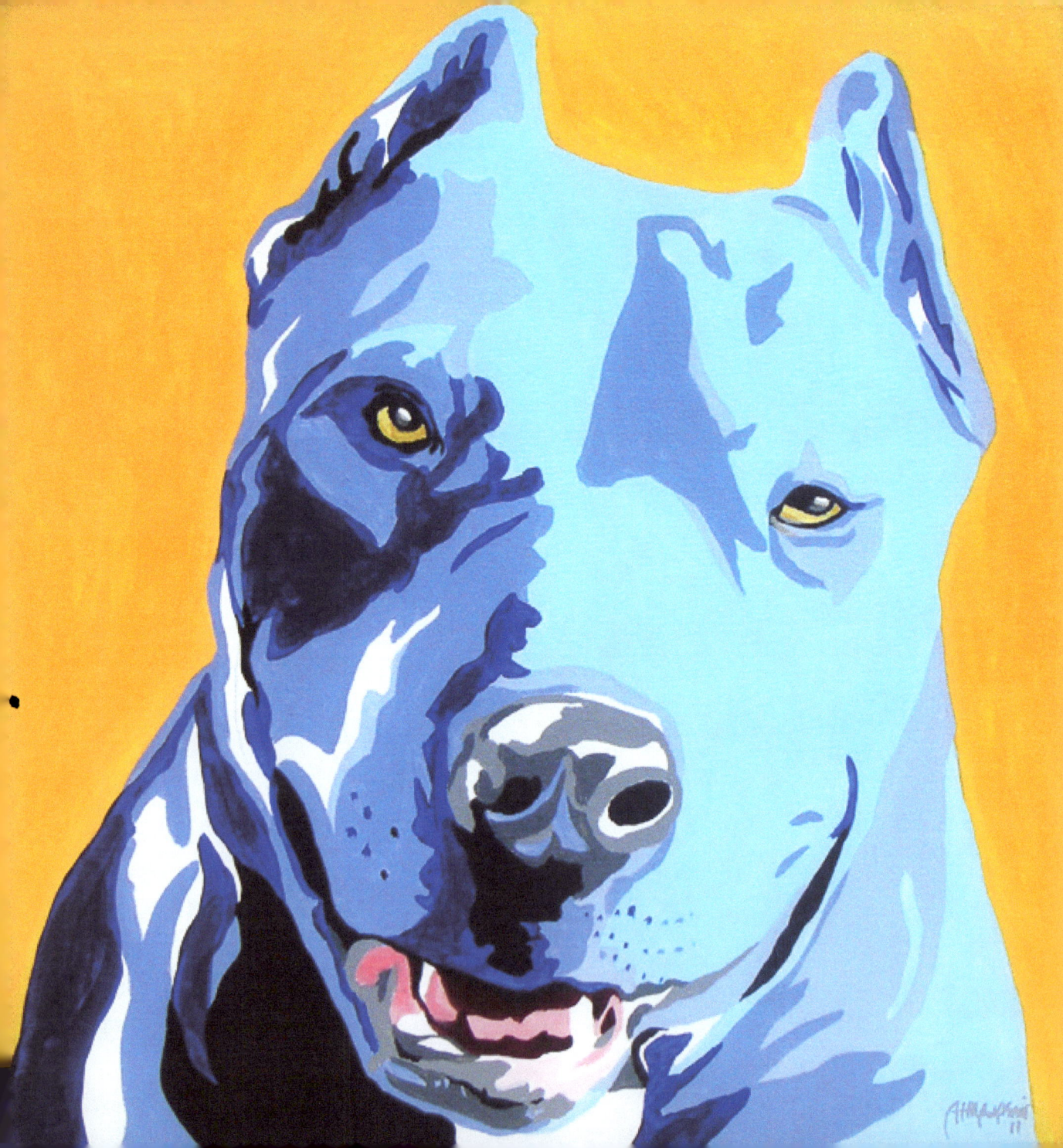

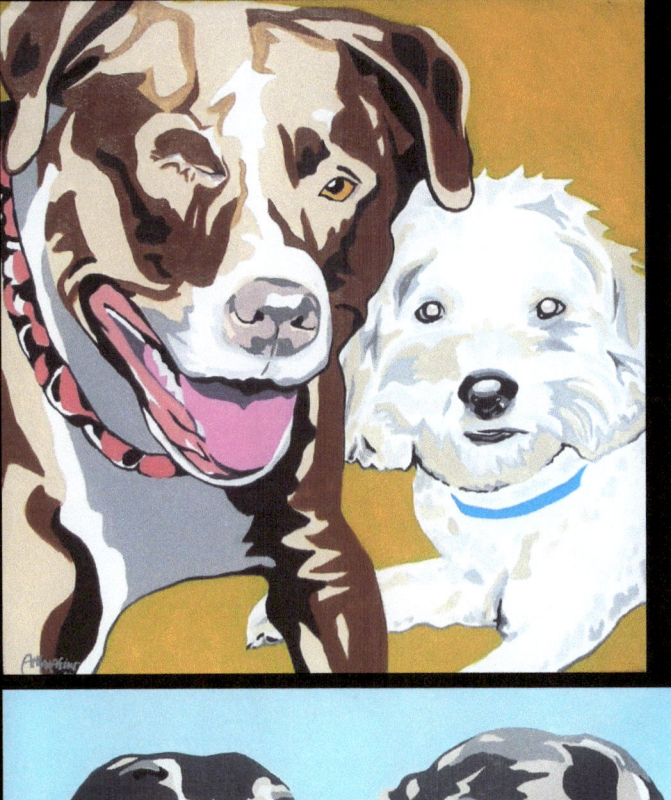
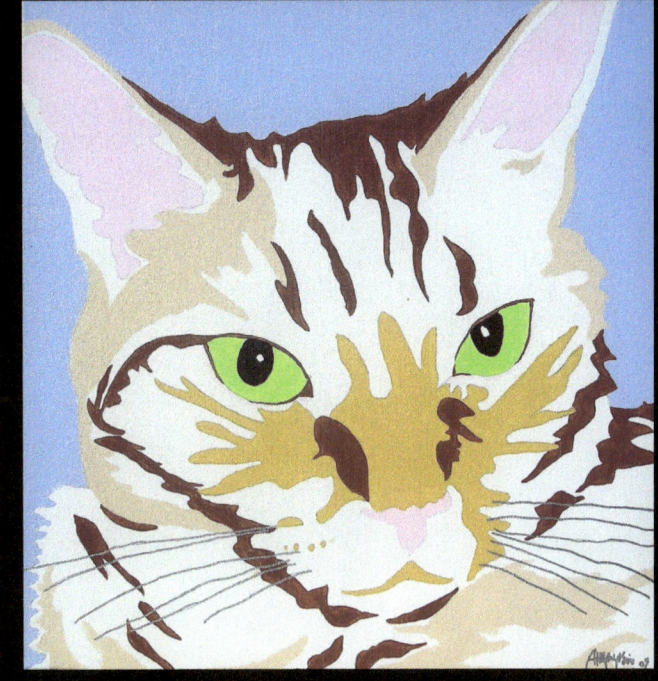
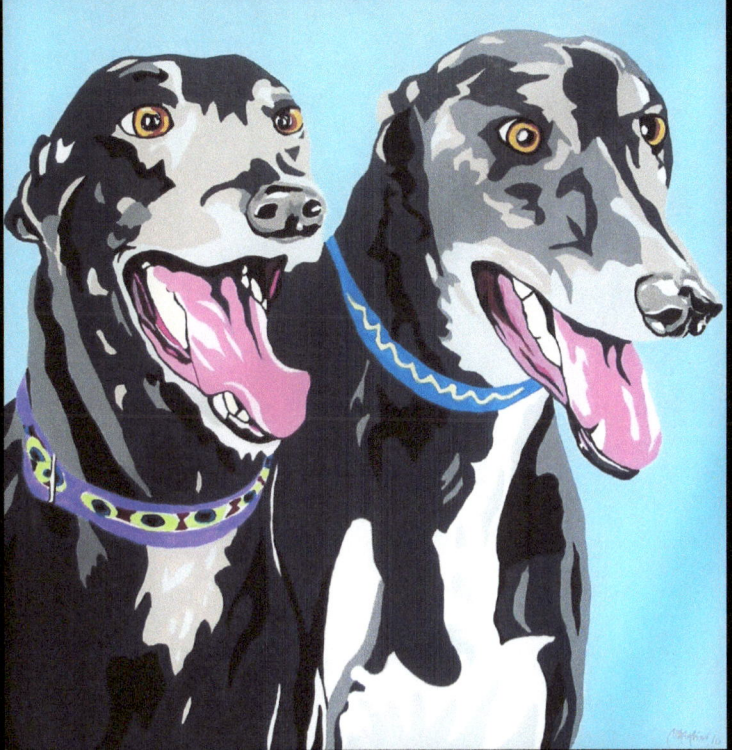
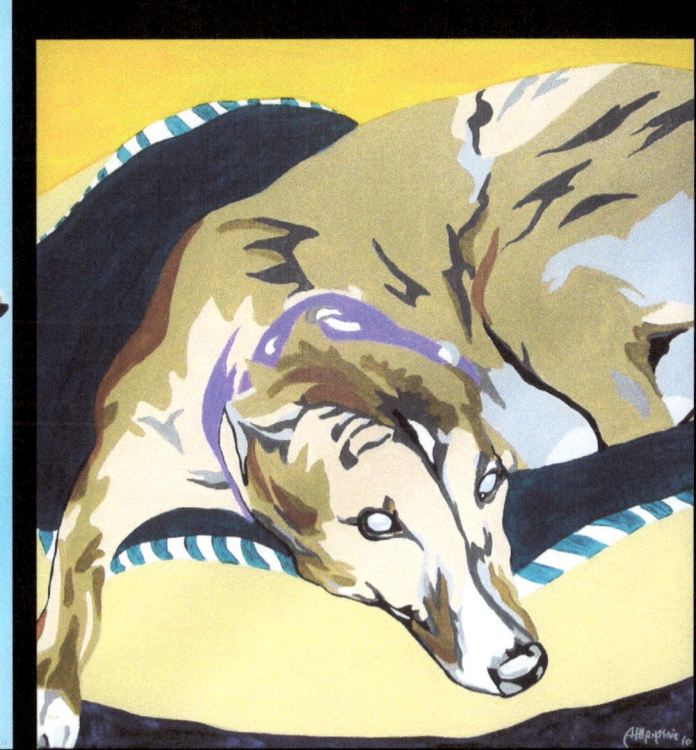

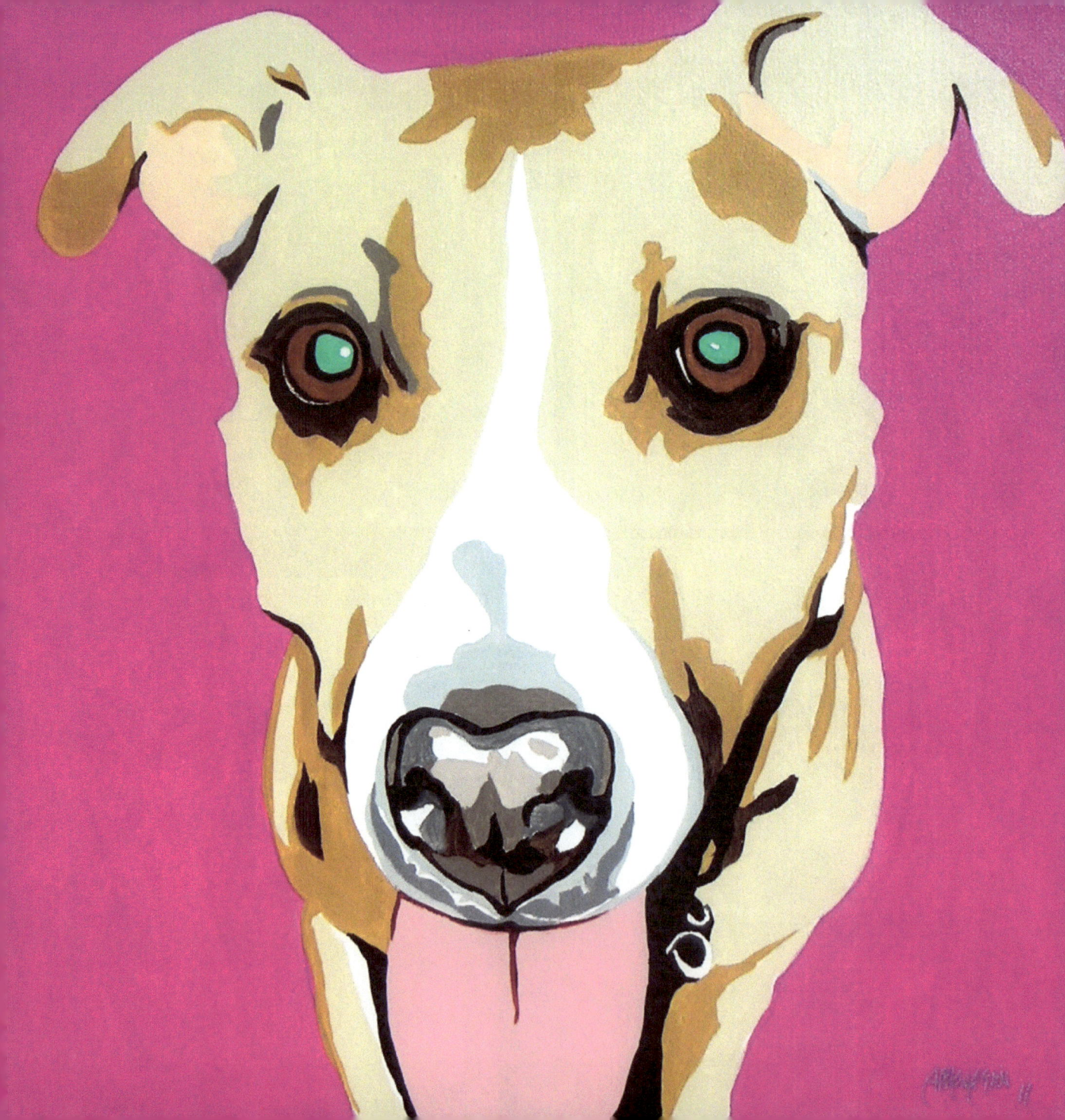

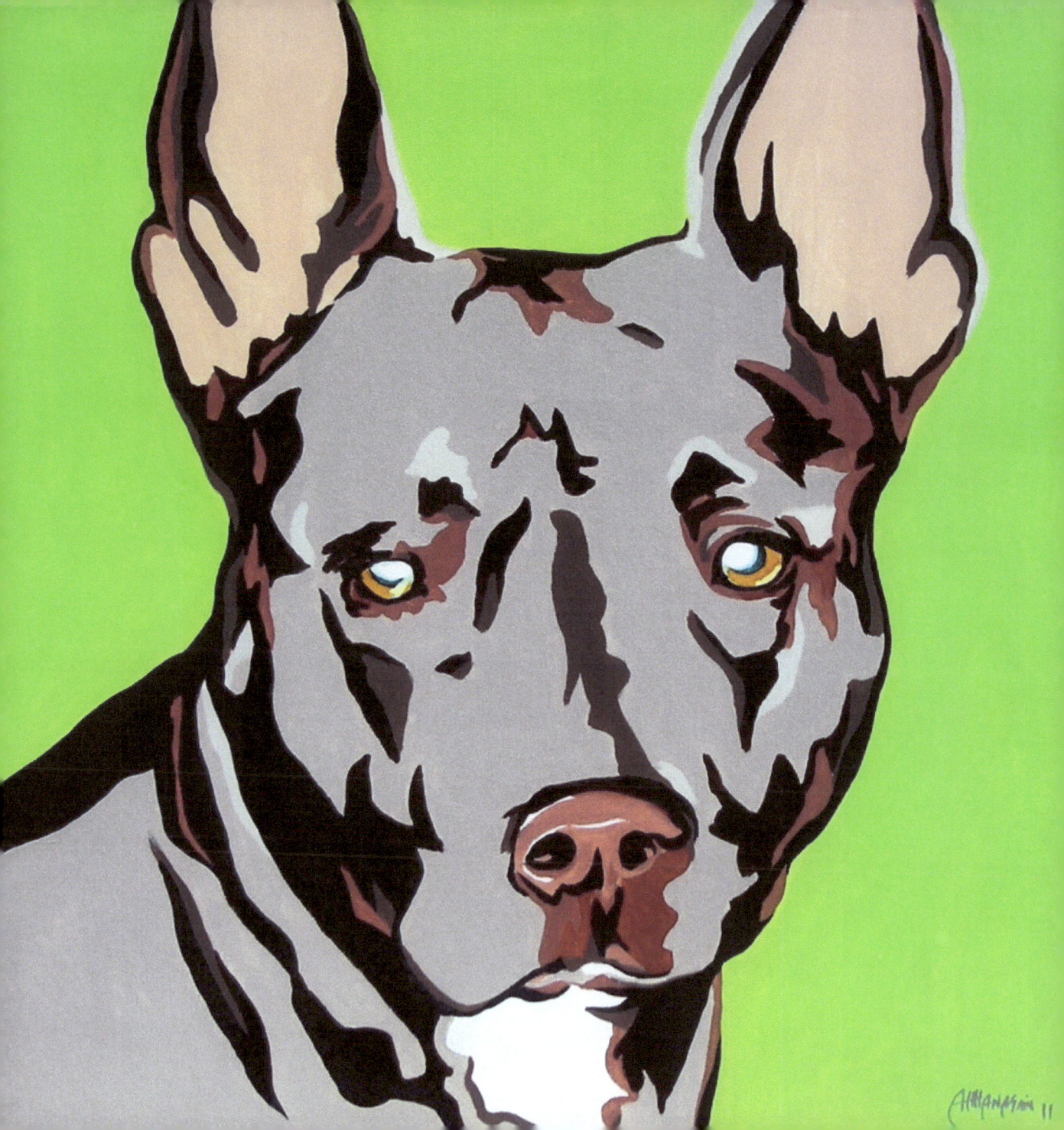

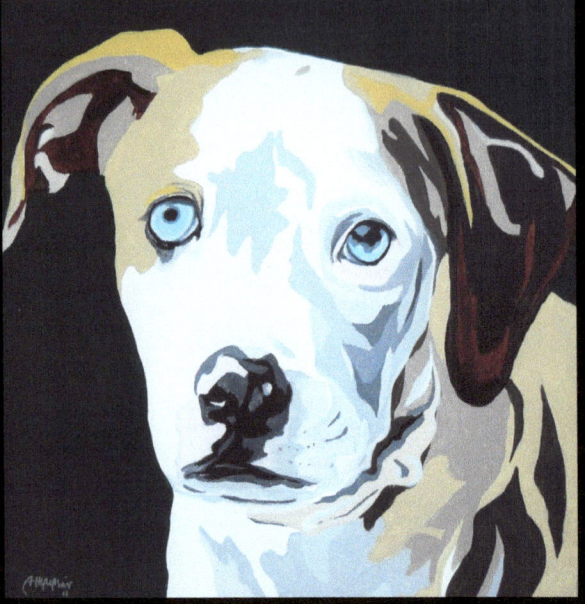

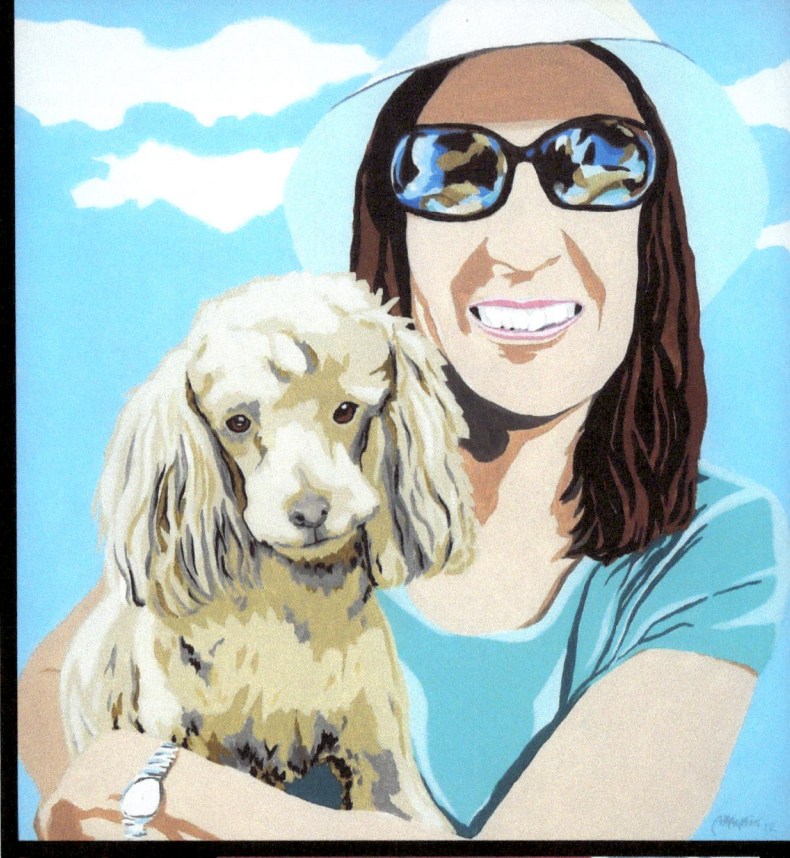

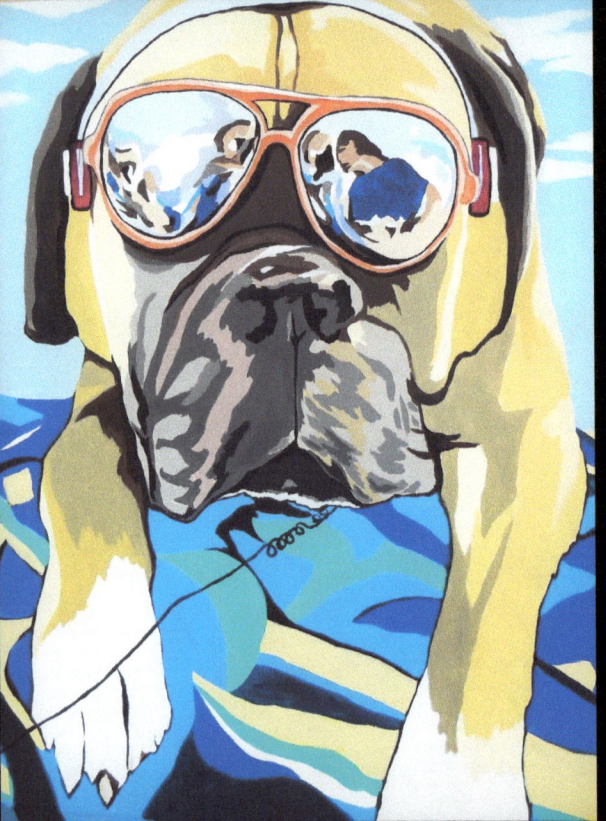

Peeps & Pet:
Portraits featuring pets along with their owners are always fun, and a challenge. I will only do these in large format, but that's what the client usually requests anyway.

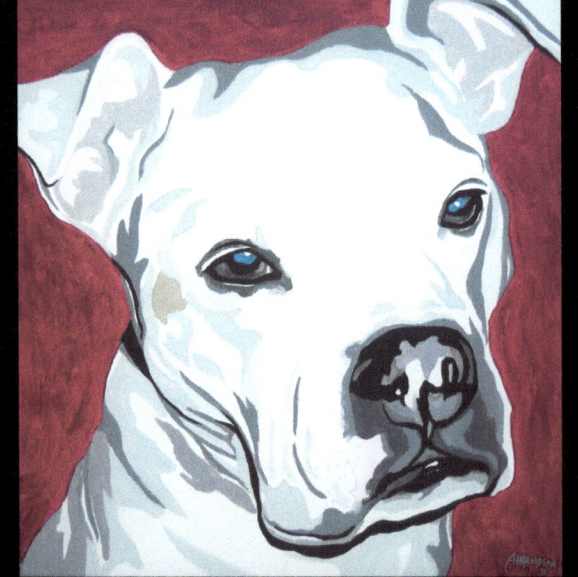

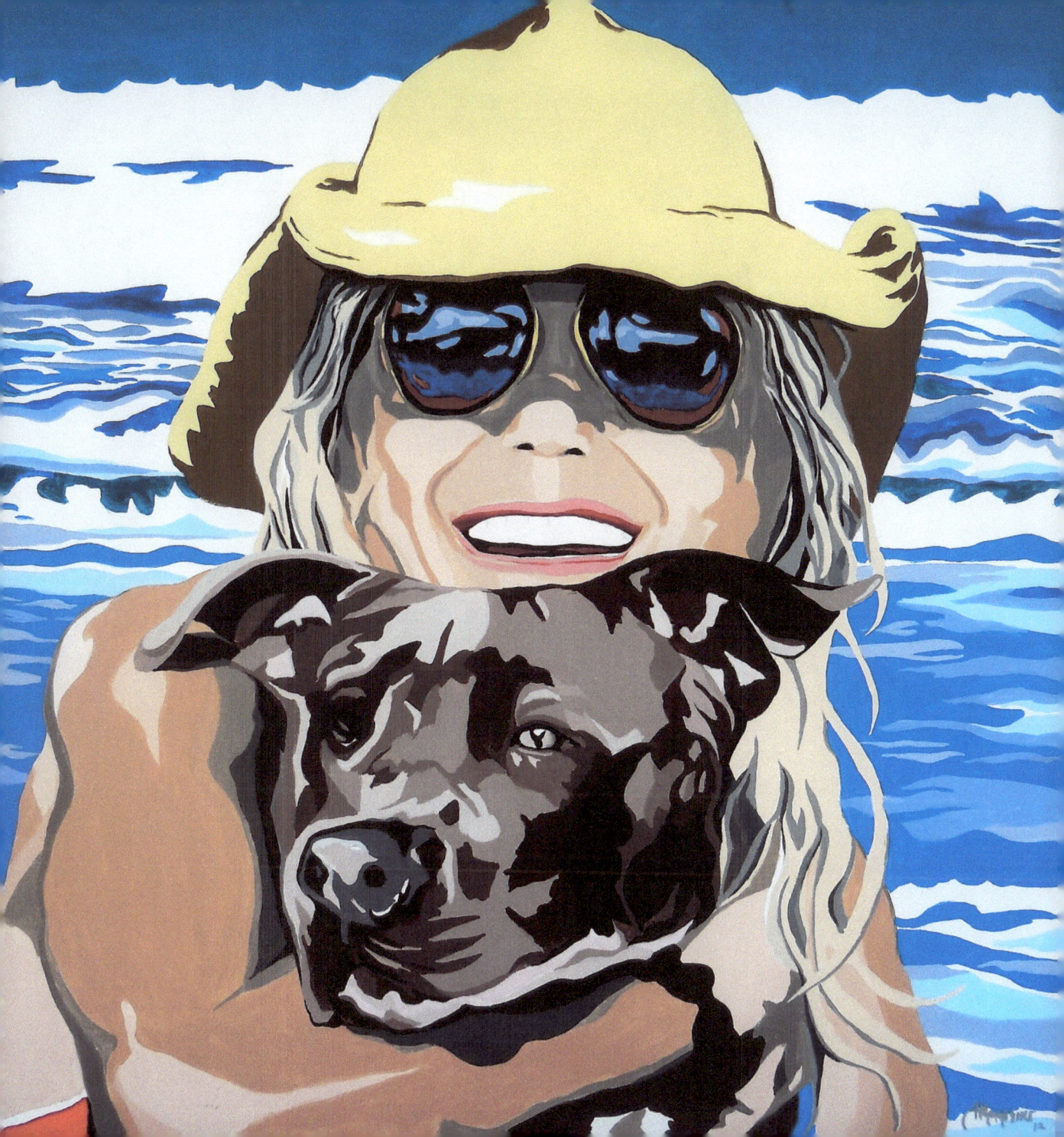

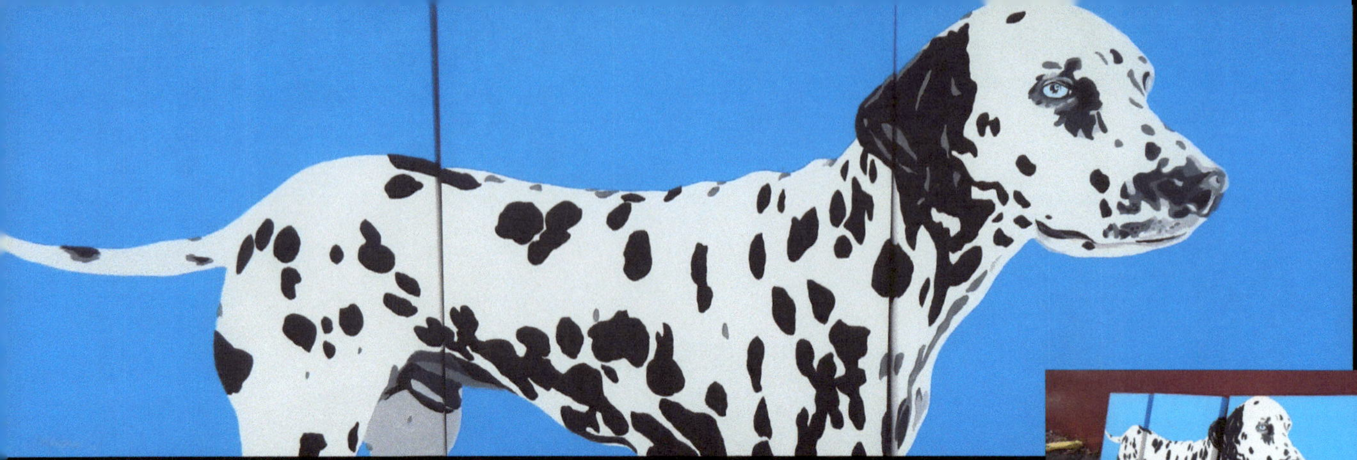

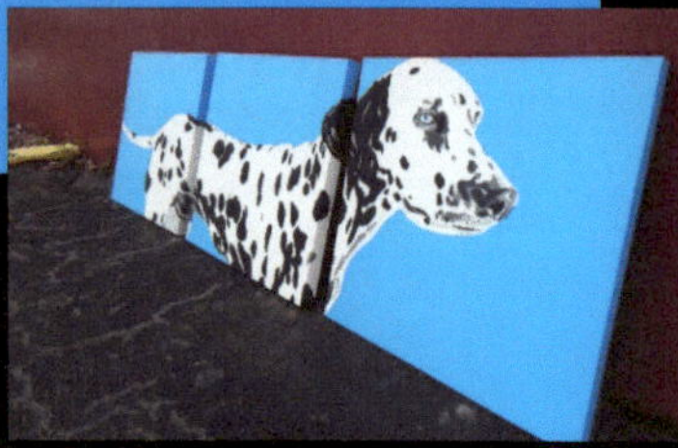

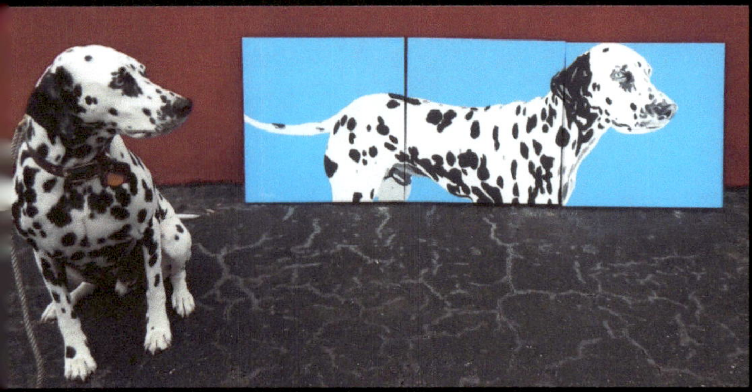

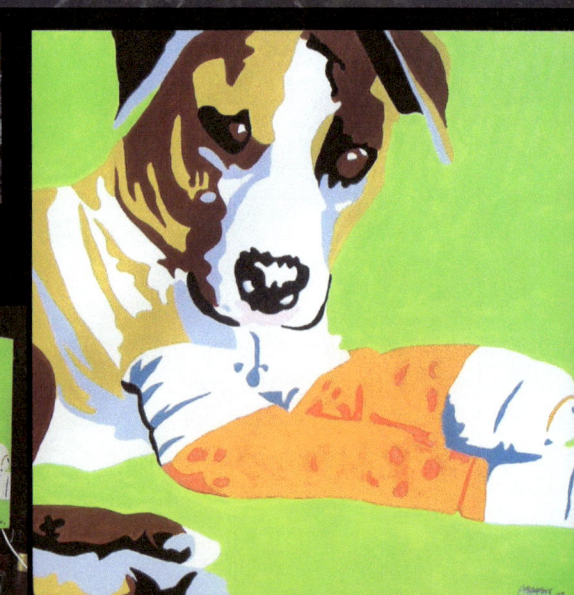

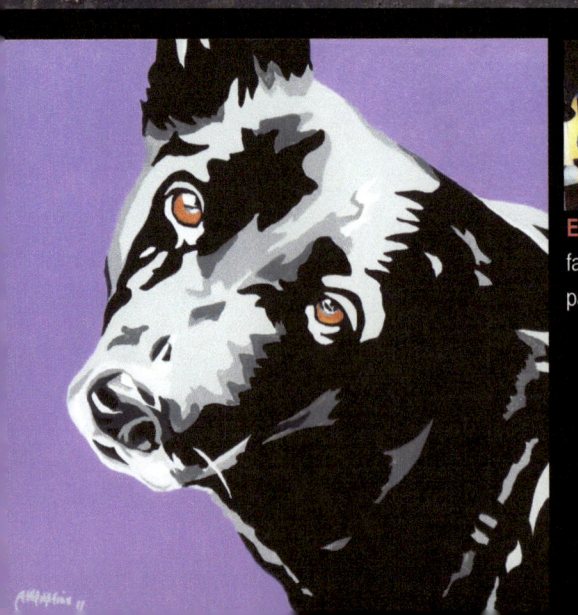

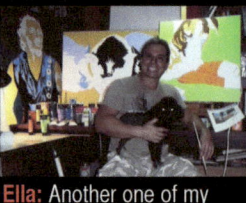

Spot On!: Sheriff the dalmatian gives a paws-up on his triptych set of canvases (that's three canvases).

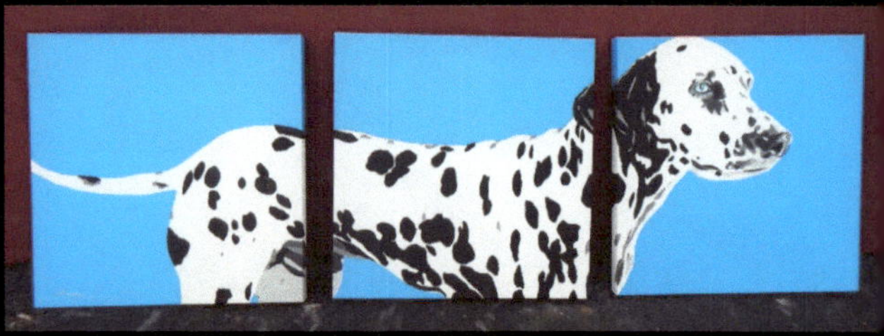

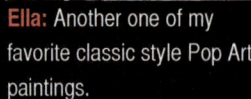

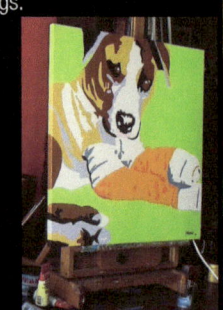

Ella: Another one of my favorite classic style Pop Art paintings.

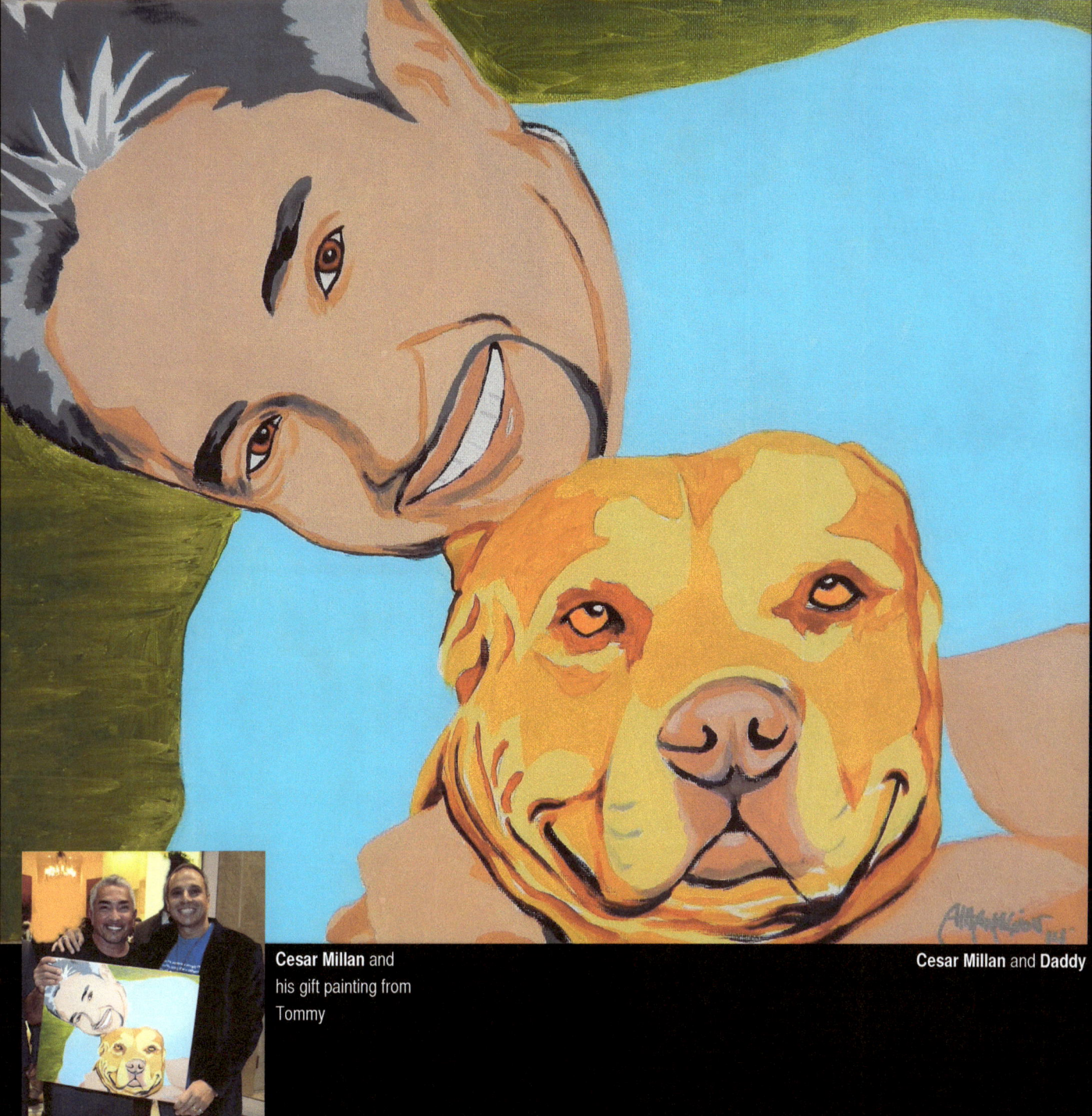

Cesar Millan and
his gift painting from
Tommy

Cesar Millan and **Daddy**

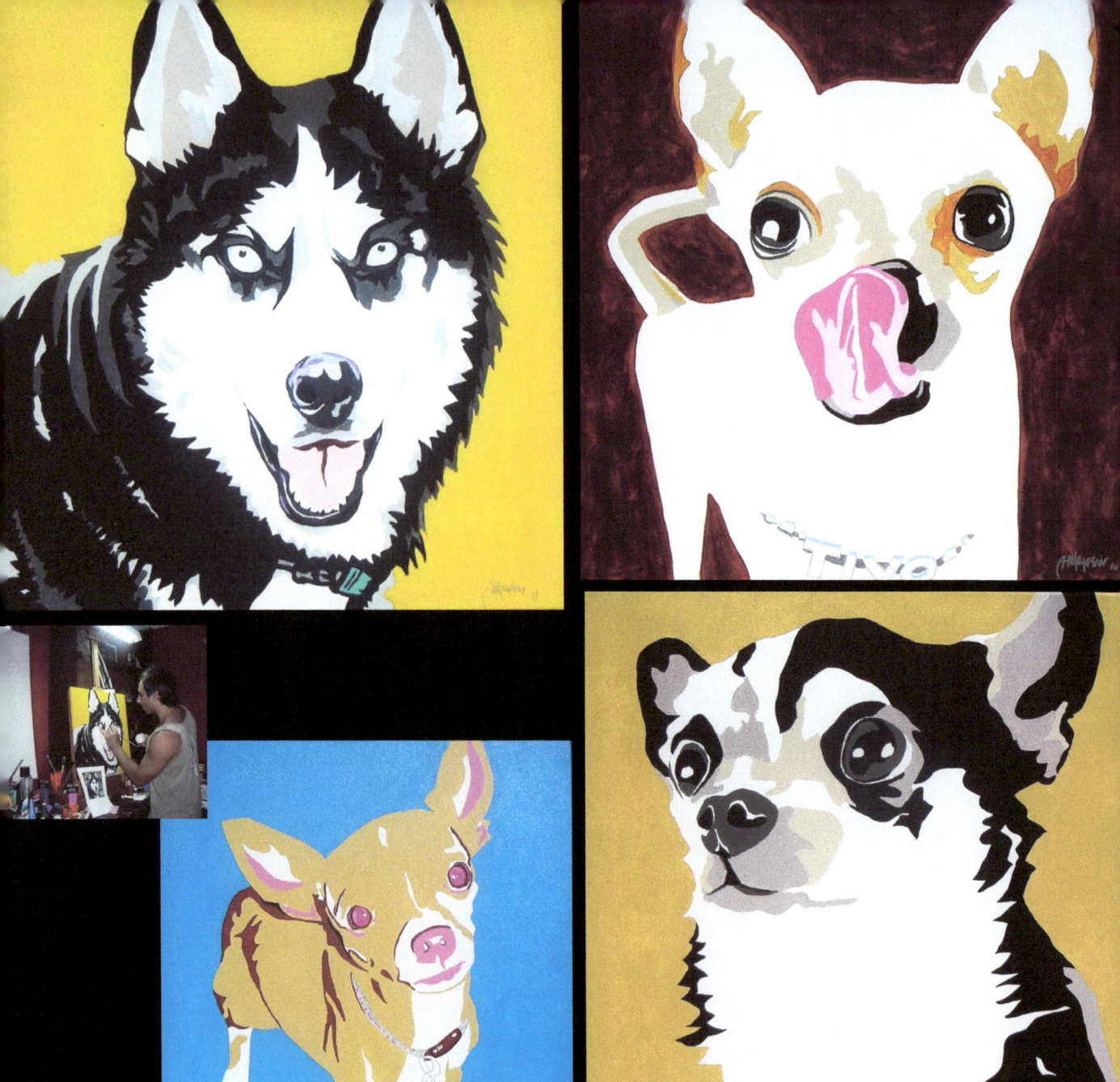

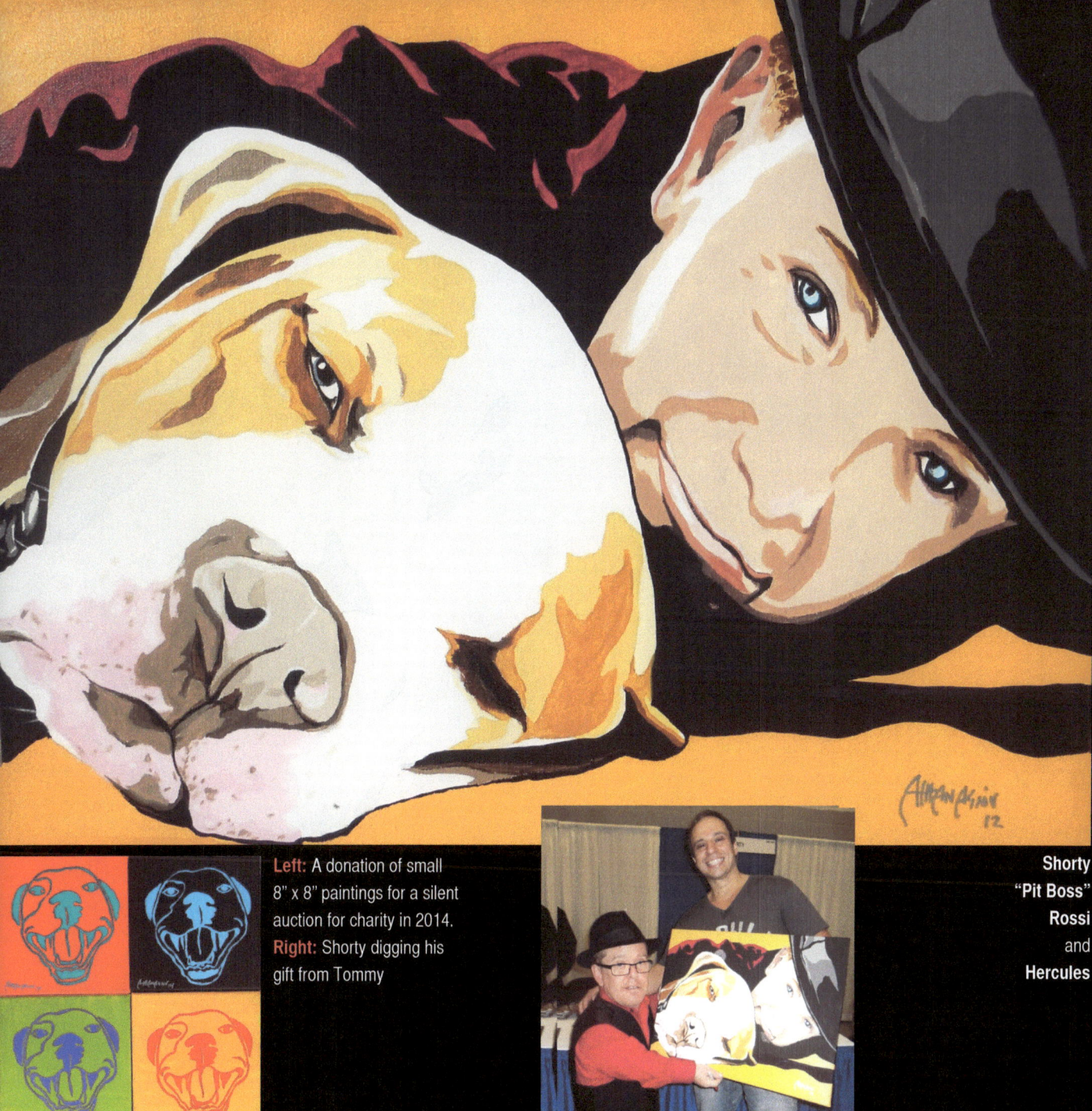

Left: A donation of small 8" x 8" paintings for a silent auction for charity in 2014. **Right:** Shorty digging his gift from Tommy

Shorty "Pit Boss" Rossi and Hercules

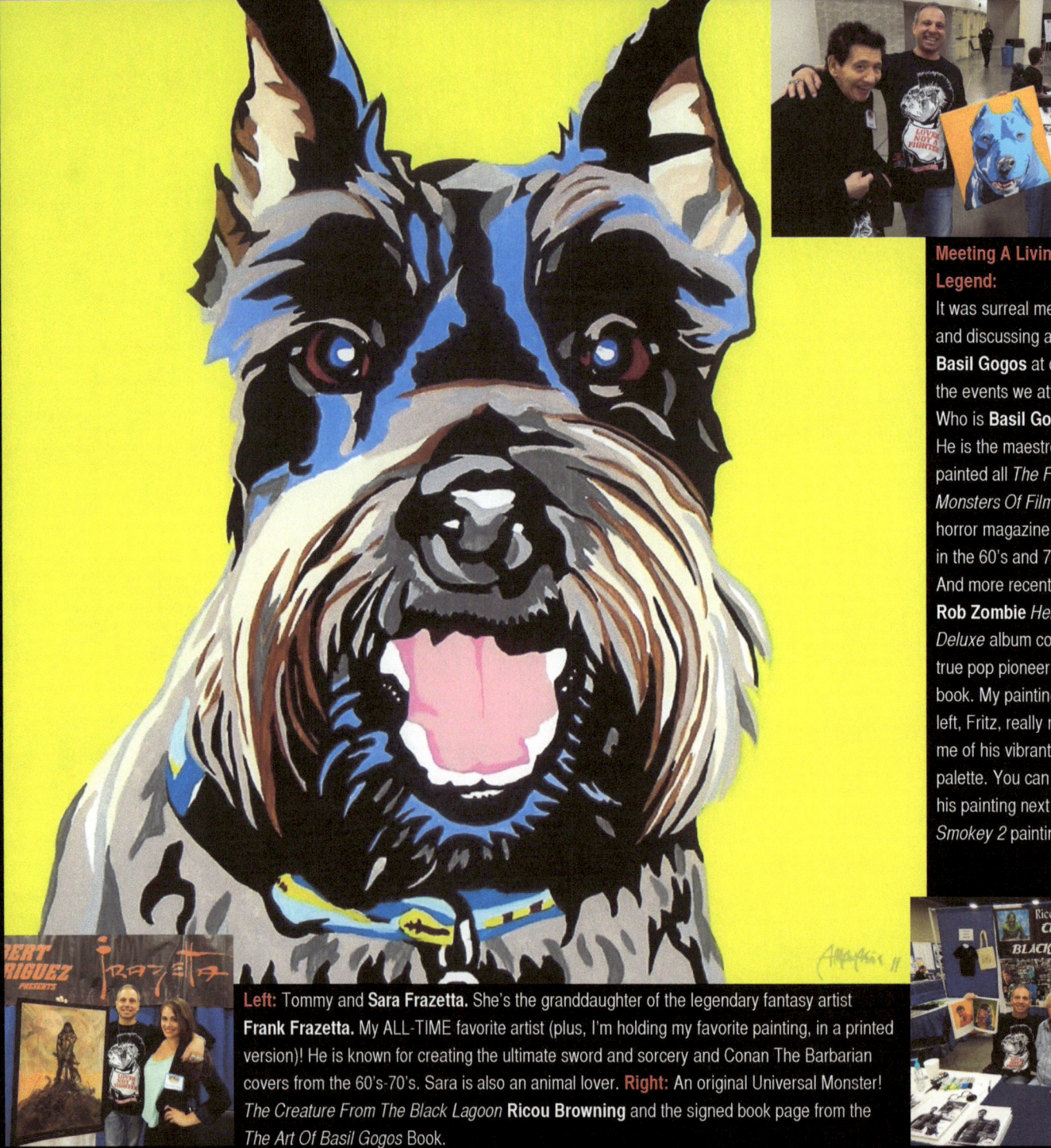

Meeting A Living Legend: It was surreal meeting and discussing art with **Basil Gogos** at one of the events we attended. Who is **Basil Gogos?** He is the maestro that painted all *The Famous Monsters Of Filmland* horror magazine covers in the 60's and 70's. And more recently, the **Rob Zombie** *Hellbilly Deluxe* album cover. A true pop pioneer in my book. My painting to the left, Fritz, really reminds me of his vibrant color palette. You can see his painting next to my *Smokey 2* painting.

Left: Tommy and **Sara Frazetta.** She's the granddaughter of the legendary fantasy artist **Frank Frazetta.** My ALL-TIME favorite artist (plus, I'm holding my favorite painting, in a printed version)! He is known for creating the ultimate sword and sorcery and Conan The Barbarian covers from the 60's-70's. Sara is also an animal lover. **Right:** An original Universal Monster! *The Creature From The Black Lagoon* **Ricou Browning** and the signed book page from the *The Art Of Basil Gogos* Book.

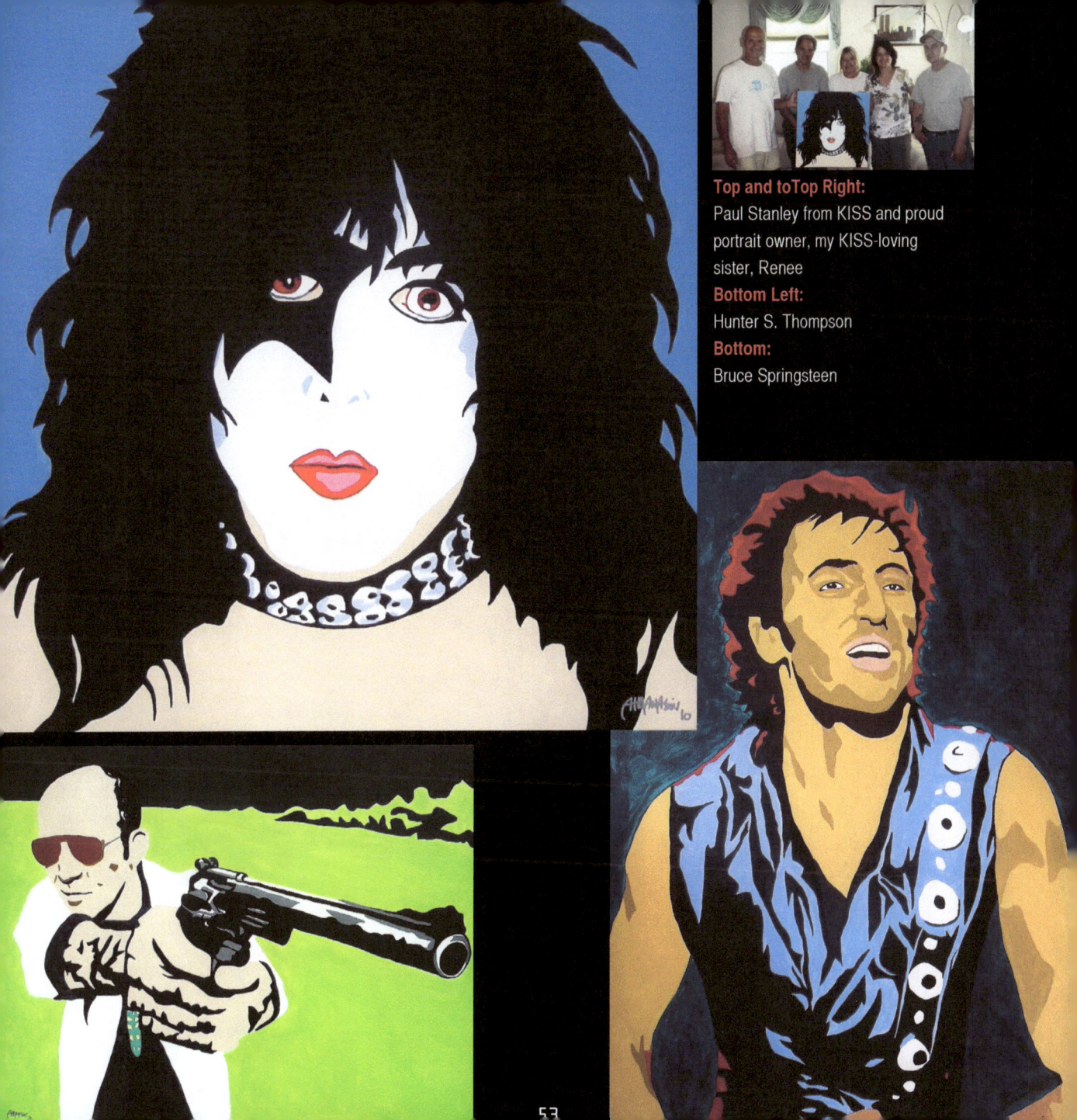

Top and toTop Right:
Paul Stanley from KISS and proud
portrait owner, my KISS-loving
sister, Renee
Bottom Left:
Hunter S. Thompson
Bottom:
Bruce Springsteen

53

PERSONAL**ART**

conic people. Man, I love doing these! I never marketed them. And I have a lot stashed away. Maybe it's time for the public to have at chance at owning these? I grabbed the first handful of my 36" x 48" canvases from the closet, lined them up, and clicked away for this portion of the book. These are the original 2008 renderings.

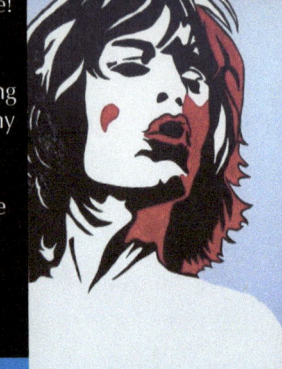

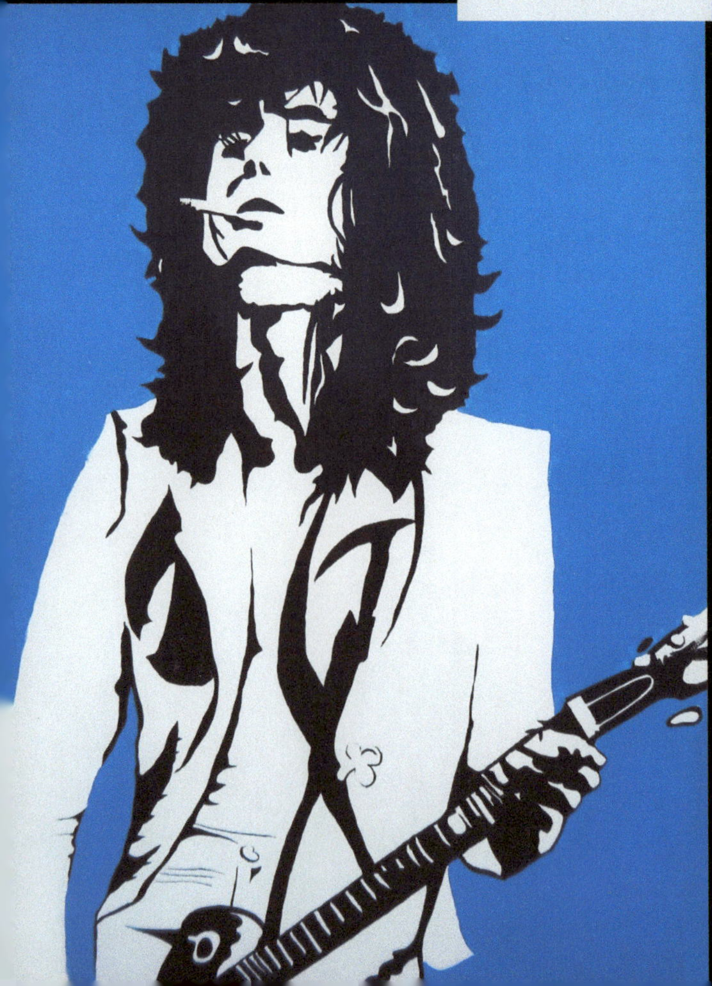

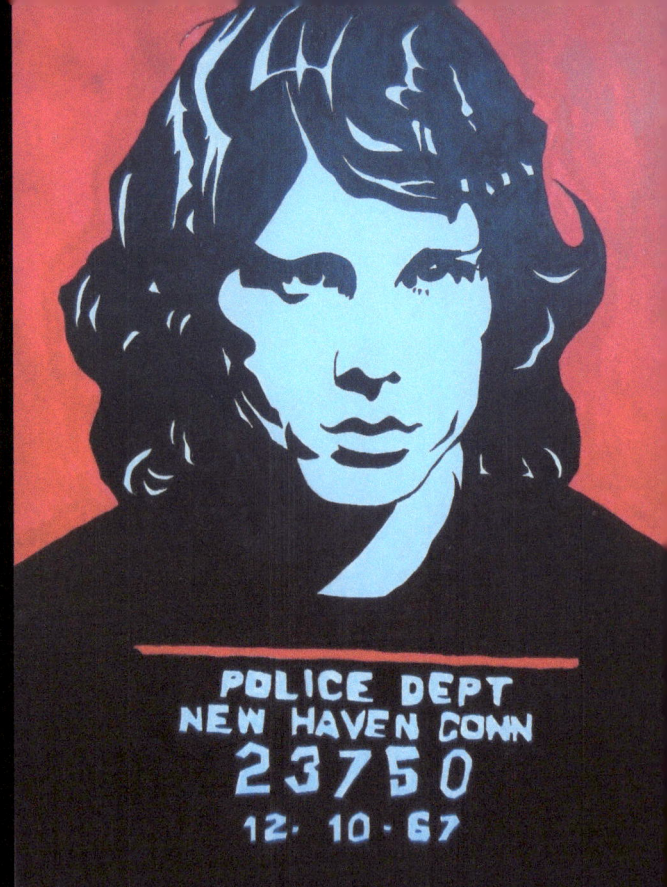

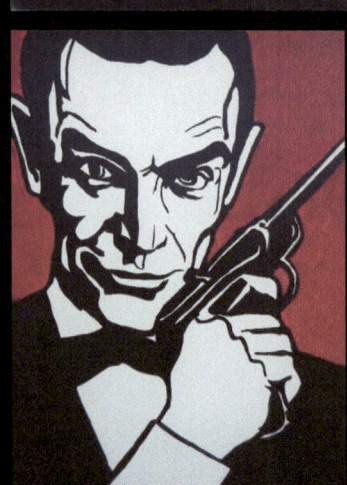

This Page: One of four Mick Jagger portraits using different colors; Jim Morrison busted; Sean Connery is James Bond; Jimmy Page

That Page: 3 stages of Elvis. I have quite a collection of him.

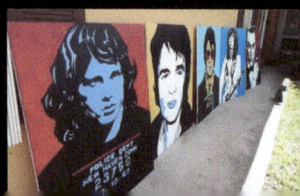

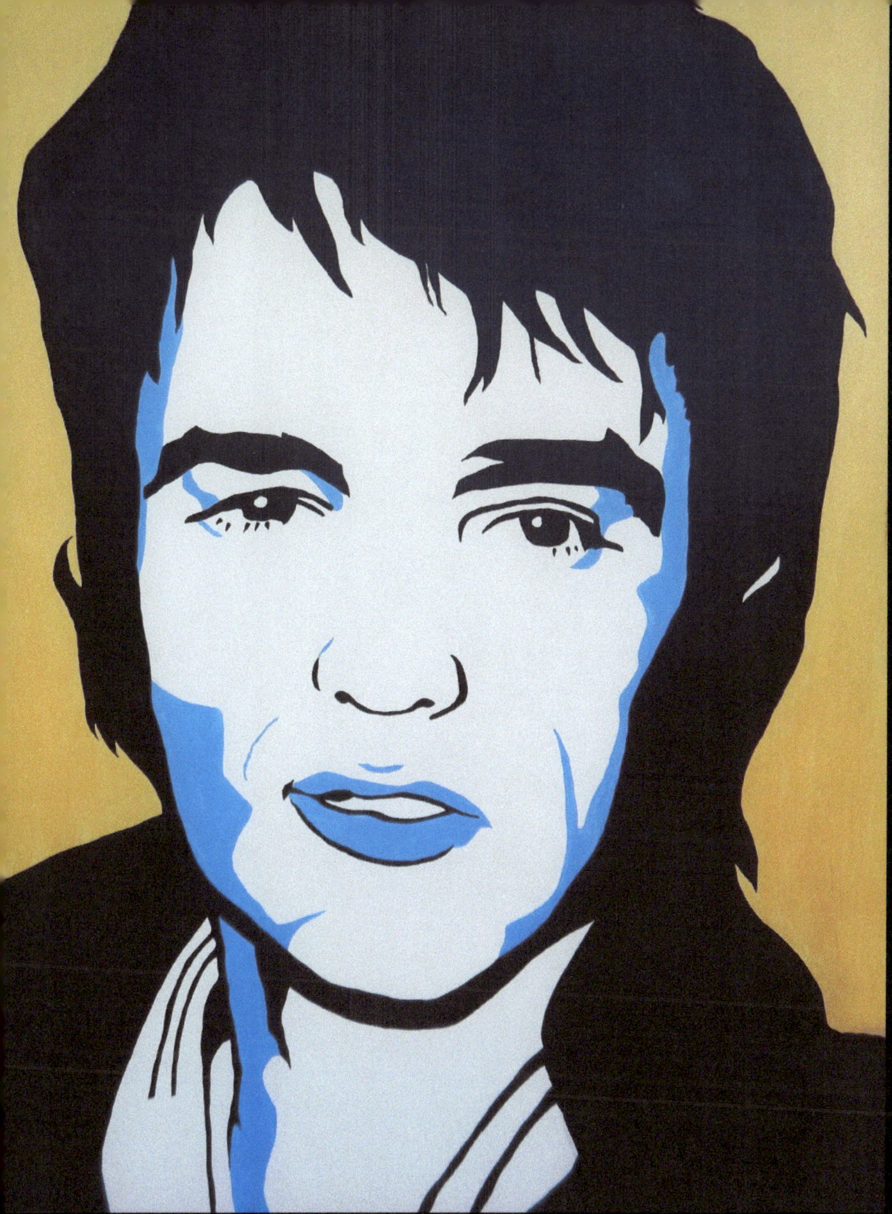

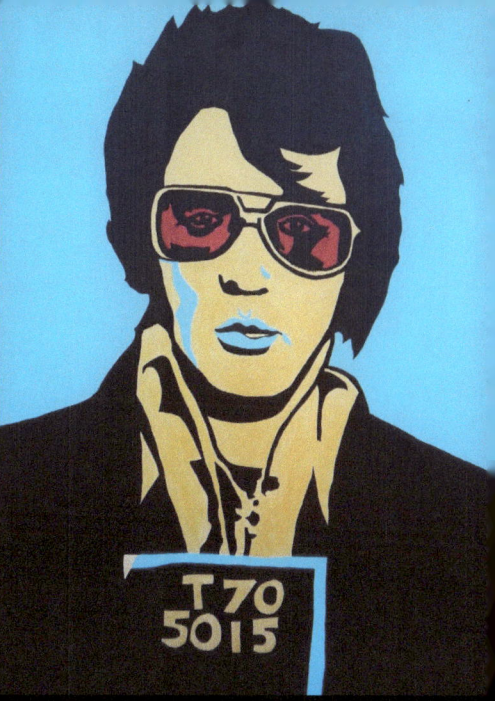
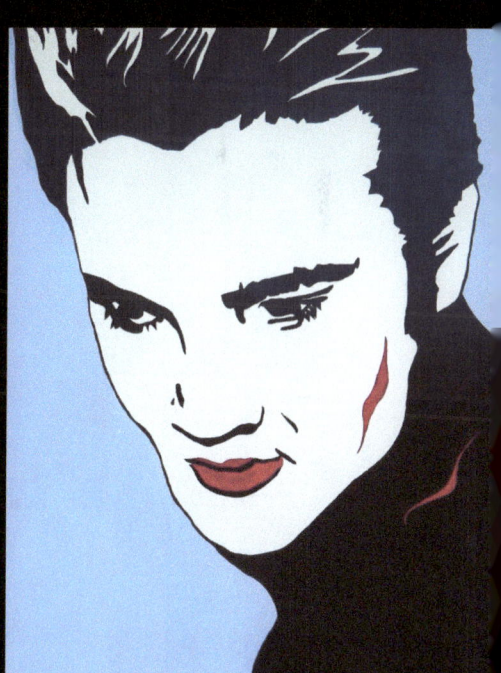

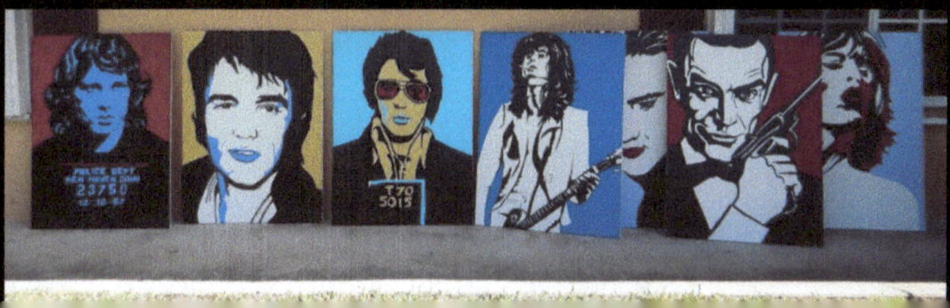

PITBULL**SHIRT**.COM

"Creative ideas happen when you try to commission paintings at a show and no one bites."

(See the bottom pic of page 6 for a visual)

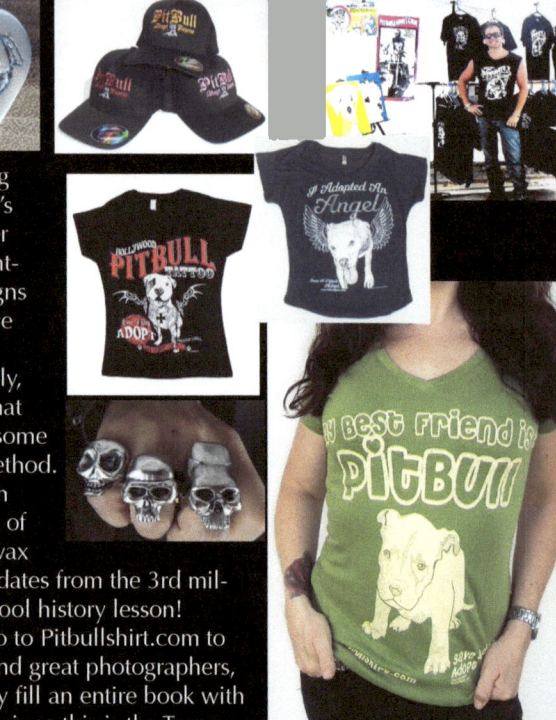

magine paying top dollar for a booth, traveling quite some distance, spending three days, long days, trying to sell your goods and not having one sale? That's when you analyze the situation. I've always wanted to create t-shirts and after being inspired by a pitbull advocacy group at that same show where my paintings brought in not a penny, we decided to create some pitbull-positive designs and see how it would go over. We started with 2 designs, and 5 years later we now have over 200 pitbull related items — shirts, hoodies, hats, natural dog treats, doggie clothing, children's books (that's the next chapter). Most recently, I thought we needed some kick-ass silver pitbull-positive jewelry (and also that Keith Richards-style Skull ring I've always wanted). After some investigation on "how to," I taught myself the lost wax method. What's that? A process of metal casting by which a molten metal is poured into a mold that's been created by means of a hand-carved wax model. Once the mold is made, the wax model is melted and drained away. The lost wax method dates from the 3rd millennium BC and has sustained few changes since then. Cool history lesson!

Now, I could display all of our designs, but you can go to Pitbullshirt.com to see that. Since we hooked up with a lot of celebs, fans, and great photographers, why not show some fun pics instead. We could absolutely fill an entire book with all the celebrity and show content we have amassed. But since this is the Tommy Pop Art "Art" book, a handful of our favorites will suffice.

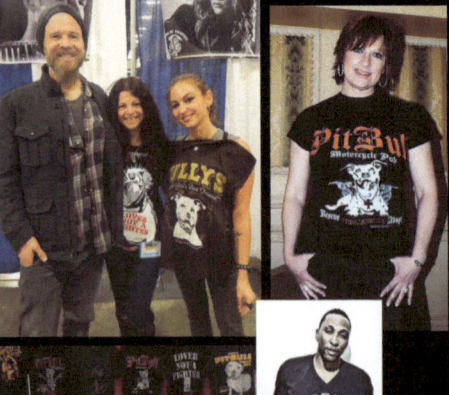

Left to Right Academy Award nominee and original *M.A.S.H* movie Hot Lips **Sally Kellerman**; Ryan **"Opie" Hurst** and **Drea "Wendy" De Matteo** of *Sons Of Anarchy* sandwiching my wife, Sharon*;* Actor and animal activist **Linda Blair**; *Real Housewives Of New Jersey's* **Caroline Manzo***;* **Shawn Marion** of the **Dallas Mavericks**; *Animal Angels*- Alexandra Paul, Michelle Harris, Kerri Kasem; Actor **Kim "Tig" Coates** of *Sons Of Anarchy;* Lights! Camera! Action! Tommy with the cast of *Animal Planet's PIT BOSS* on a season finale episode.

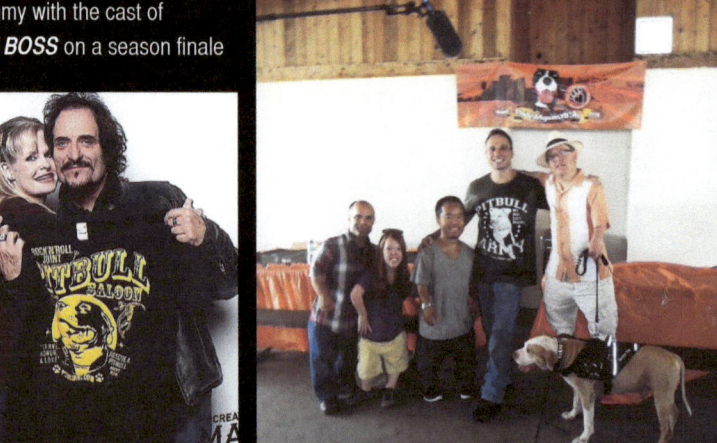

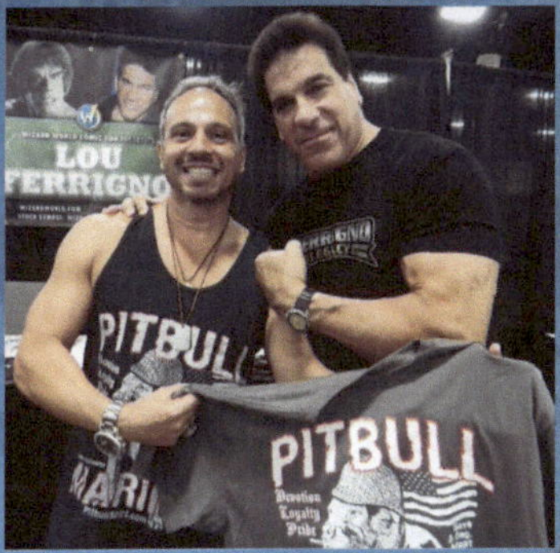

The HULK **Lou Ferrigno**

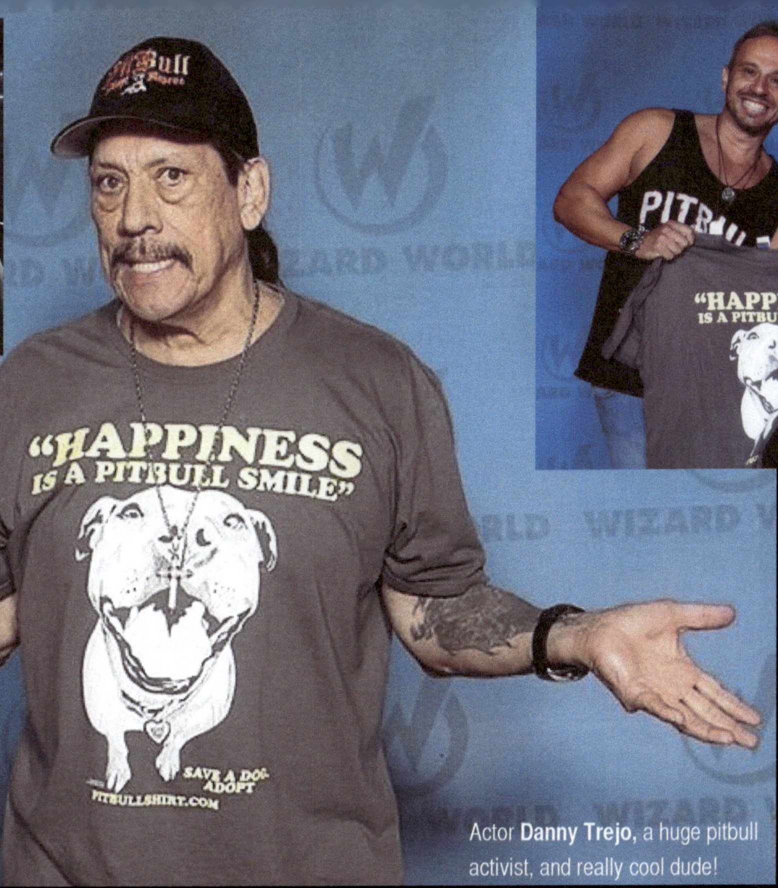

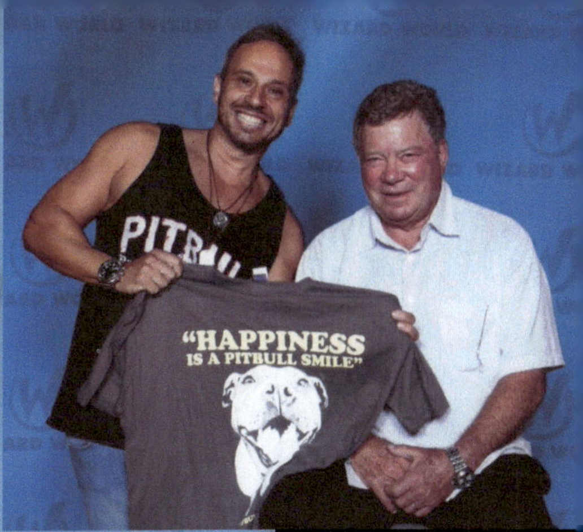

I just got beamed up to the Starship Enterprise! Legend **William Shatner**

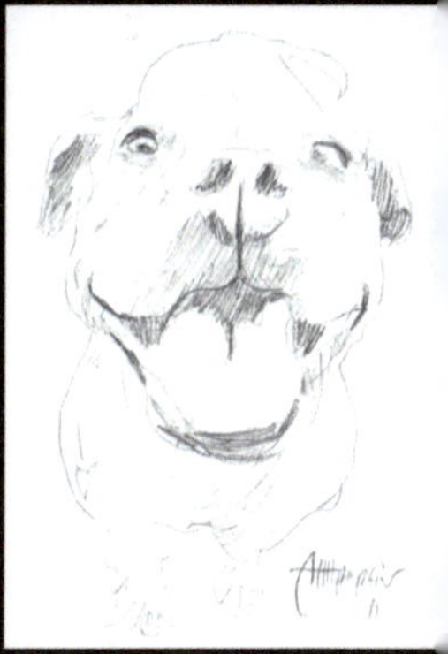

Actor **Danny Trejo,** a huge pitbull activist, and really cool dude!

Original pencil sketch

Left to Right Actor **Kristen Bauer** of HBO's *True Blood; The Walking Dead's* Scott "Hershel" Wilson; Norman "Daryl" Reedus; Tia Maria Torres of *Animal Planet's Pit Bulls and Parolees*

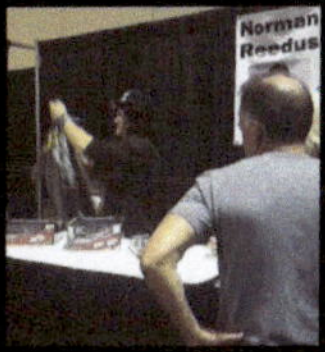

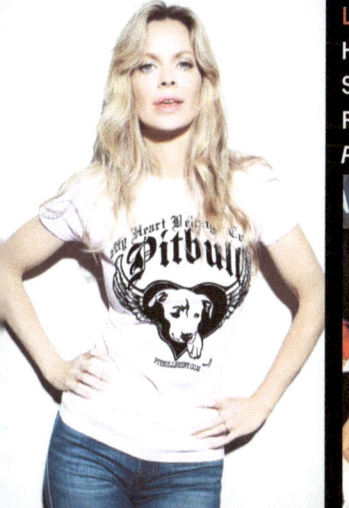

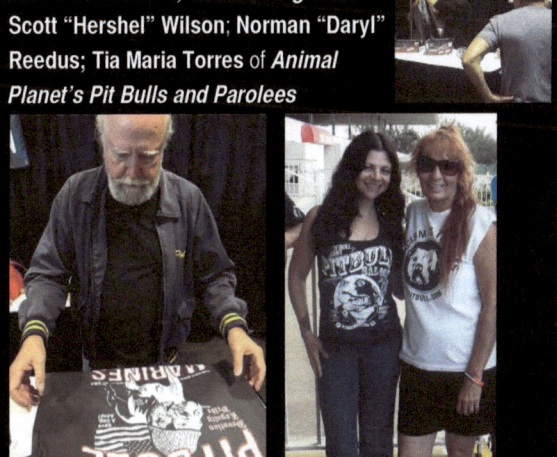

"HAPPINESS IS A PITBULL SMILE"

The beginning of 2011. Time to create some new designs for the spring. Let me think. How about the slogan, "HAPPINESS IS A PITBULL SMILE'?

You hear it from a lot of artists and musicians: "It just came to me. Floated right into my mind." Yep, that was my scenerio too. Poof! I even had the font pictured. Next was the drawing. A quick pencil sketch (see above), then traced over in pen & ink, scanned, designed and sent off to the screen printers. Our most popular, best-selling design since its launch!

CHILDREN'S**BOOKS**

t was little Bailey The Mouse who got the author/illustrator ball rolling. That cute adventurer was my original children's story. I began illustrating it in 2006. Working on 36 full-color oil paintings was a task, but it's always a pleasure to visualize, then create your idea. It was great, but I really had no outlet to promote, and trying to get this published is like winning the million dollar Lotto. Into the closet it went.

Around 2012, I had the idea for a pitbull-themed children's book. Focusing on rescue, adoption, and the unfair practice of dog breed discrimination, I tailored it for the young reader. I came up with the story to tie these elements in and gave it that early 70's style *School House Rock* look. I love the 70's. Now I had the means to get it to the public with the invention of self-publishing, and had a targeted outlet with our PitbullShirt.com fan base. Late November we launched *Peanut The Pitbull,* followed by *Peanut's First Snowy Christmas* a month later. Tahdaa! These books sold! And still do. I decided to make an edited version for the even younger kids (teaching about

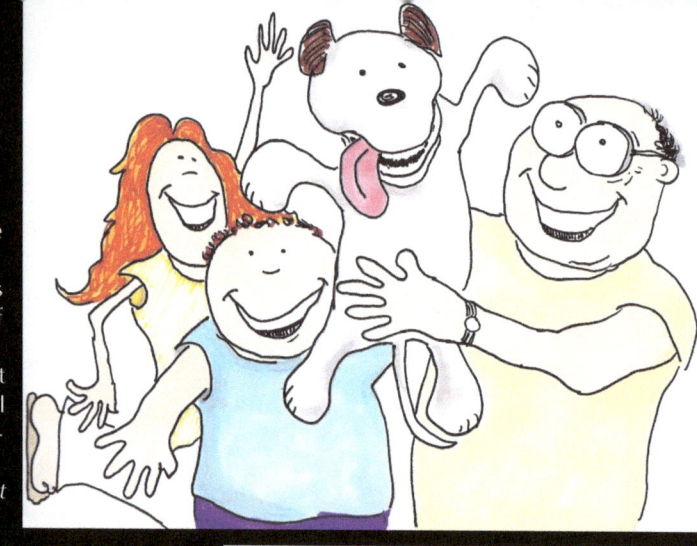

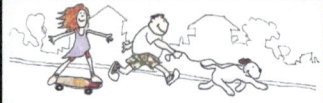

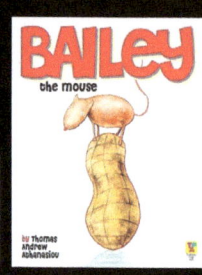

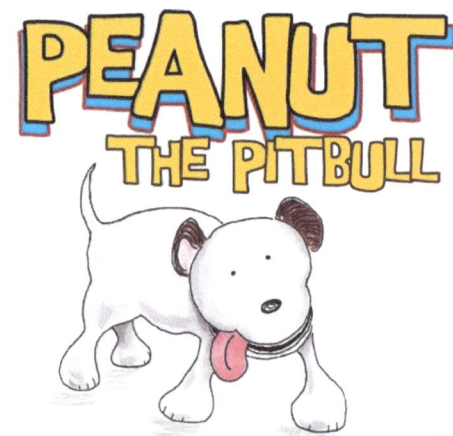

by Thomas Andrew Athanasiou

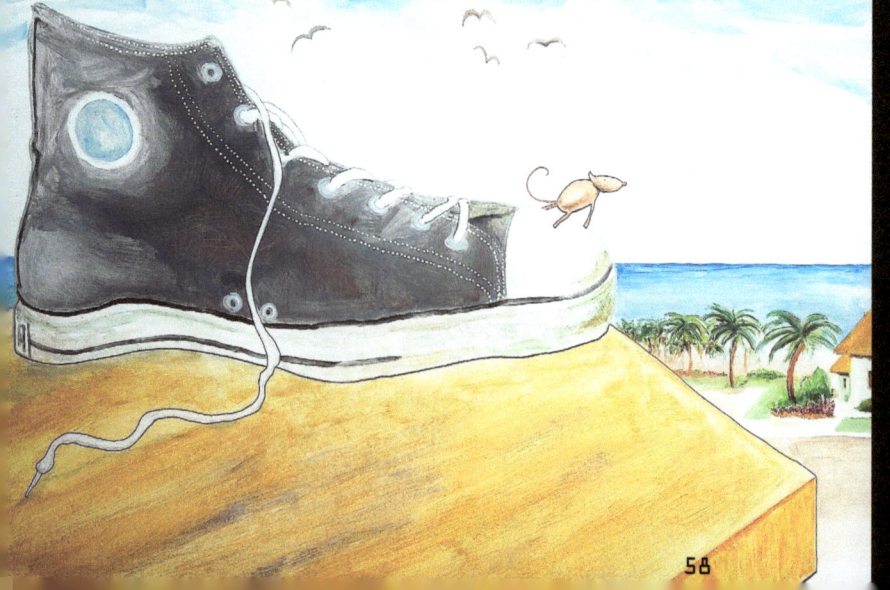

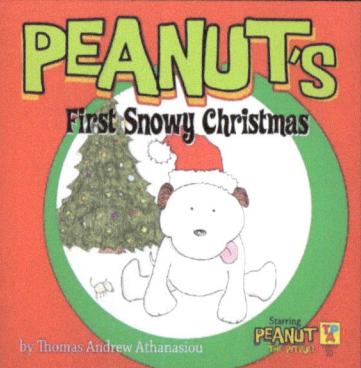

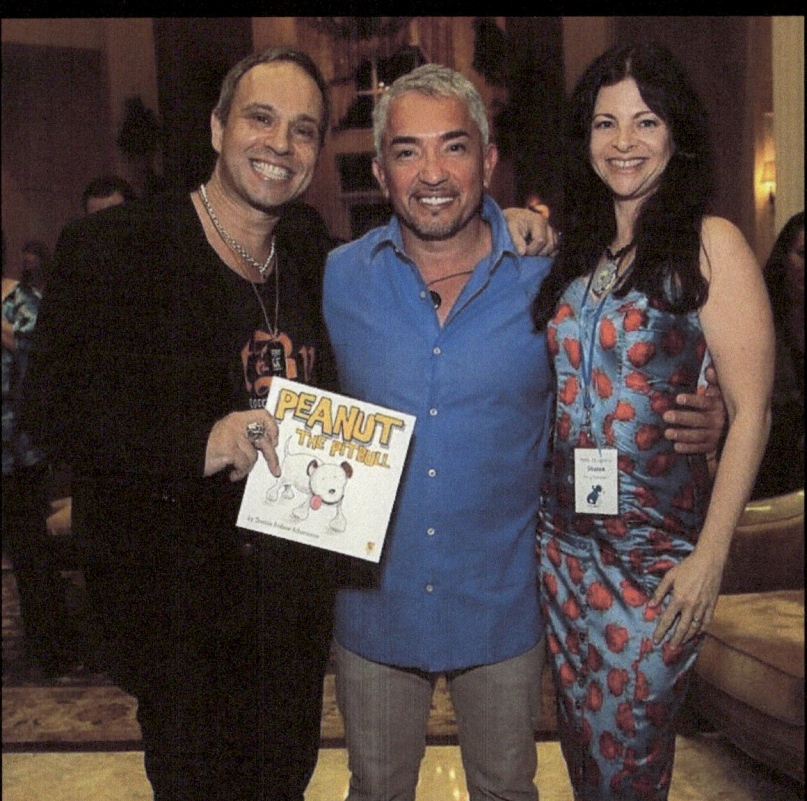

An honor! Tommy, **Cesar Millan,** Sharon

compassion should start young, very young), and have versions printed in French, Spanish, and German. Peanut's next book, *Peanut's Summer Vacation,* is slated for early 2016. And Bailey? Well, he made his guest appearances in the Peanut books, which finally gave the green light to get his book published.

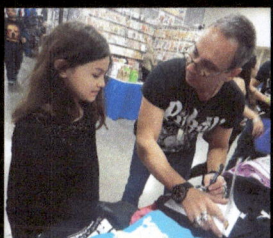
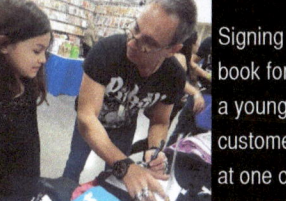

Signing a book for a young customer at one of our events.

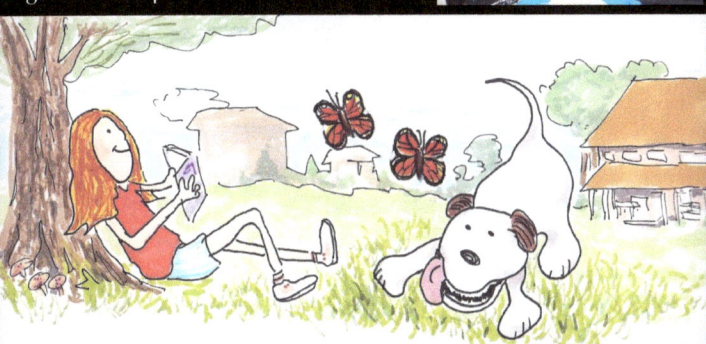

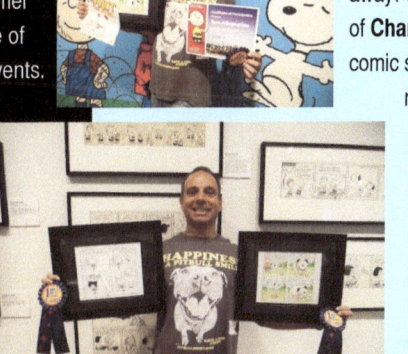

My Biggest Thrill

Florida Comic Strip Challenge
August 28 – September 7

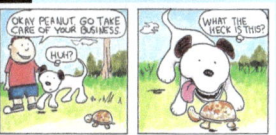
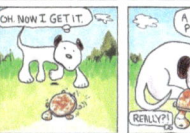
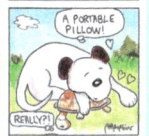

Receiving the award for **BEST FLORIDA COMIC STRIP** at the **Charles M. Schulz** *'Peanuts In Pop Culture'* exhibit in Hollywood, FL, for my "**Little Mean Vanilla Bean**" comic, and also winning another 1st Place for **BEST COMIC STRIP** Award for my "**Peanut The Pitbull**" comic strip in the Organization/Business category really blew me away! Winning in the presence of **Charles M. Schulz'** original comic strips was surreal. Sharon said I almost passed out when we entered the gallery room and I saw the 1st Place ribbons on both of my pieces. I have to say that I really *was* about drop! I think a **Vanilla Bean** comic strip is next on the agenda...

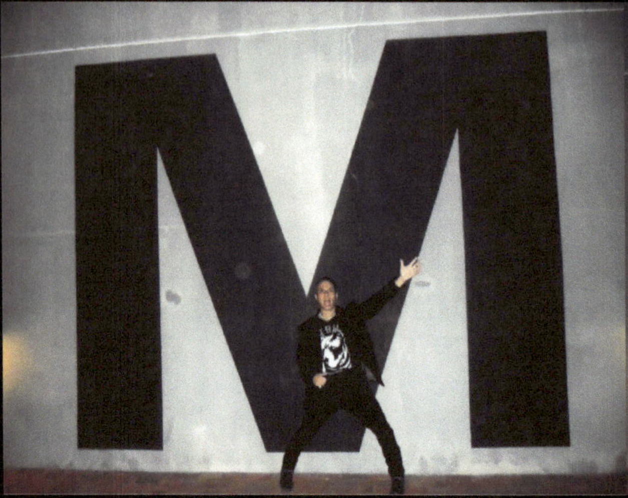

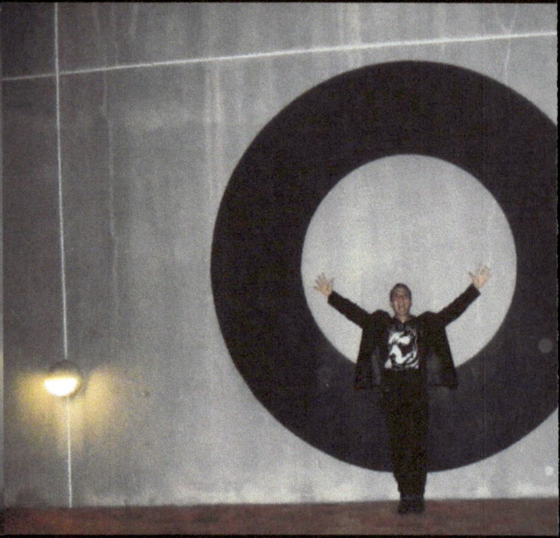

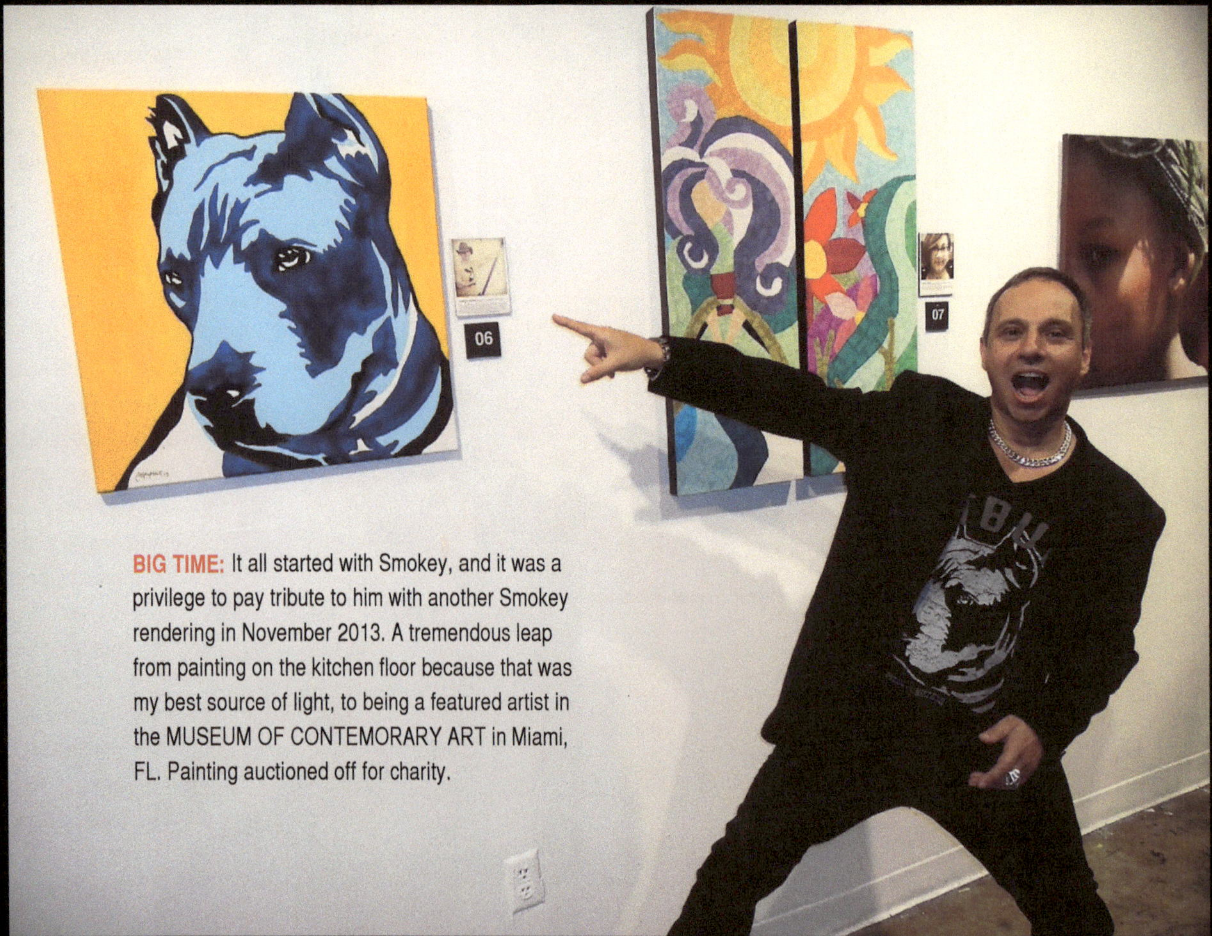

BIG TIME: It all started with Smokey, and it was a privilege to pay tribute to him with another Smokey rendering in November 2013. A tremendous leap from painting on the kitchen floor because that was my best source of light, to being a featured artist in the MUSEUM OF CONTEMORARY ART in Miami, FL. Painting auctioned off for charity.

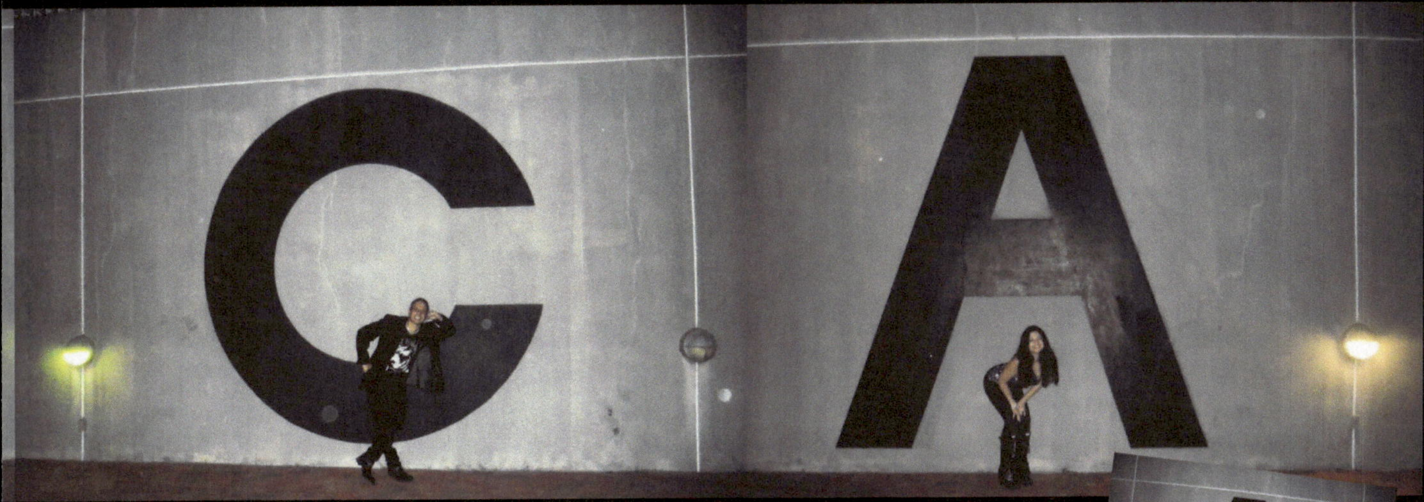

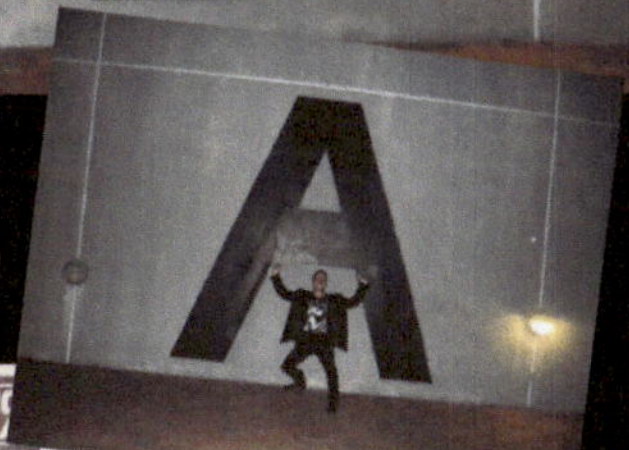

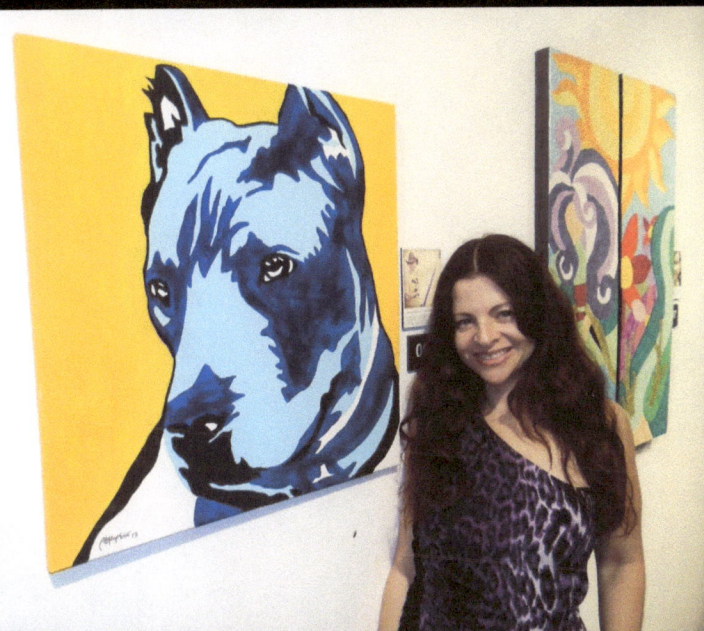

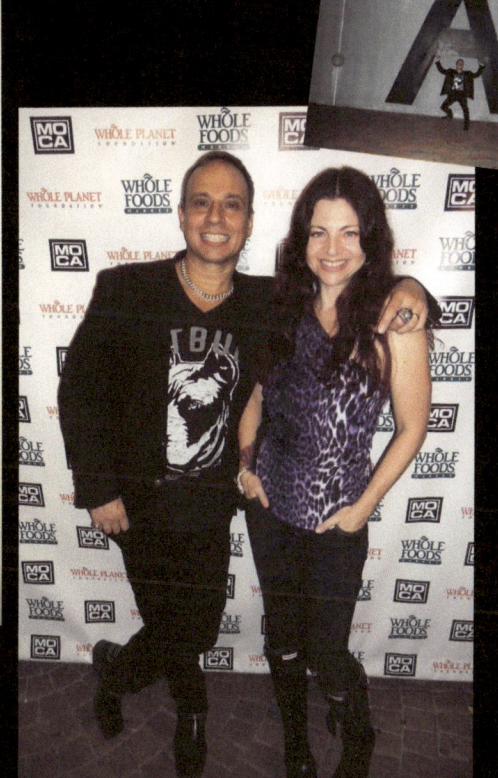

...THE**GRAND**FINALE?

N ah. Just another chance to create more art for the second edition of this book! Let's see where the yellow brick road of pop art takes us...

Tommy and Sharon on the red carpet

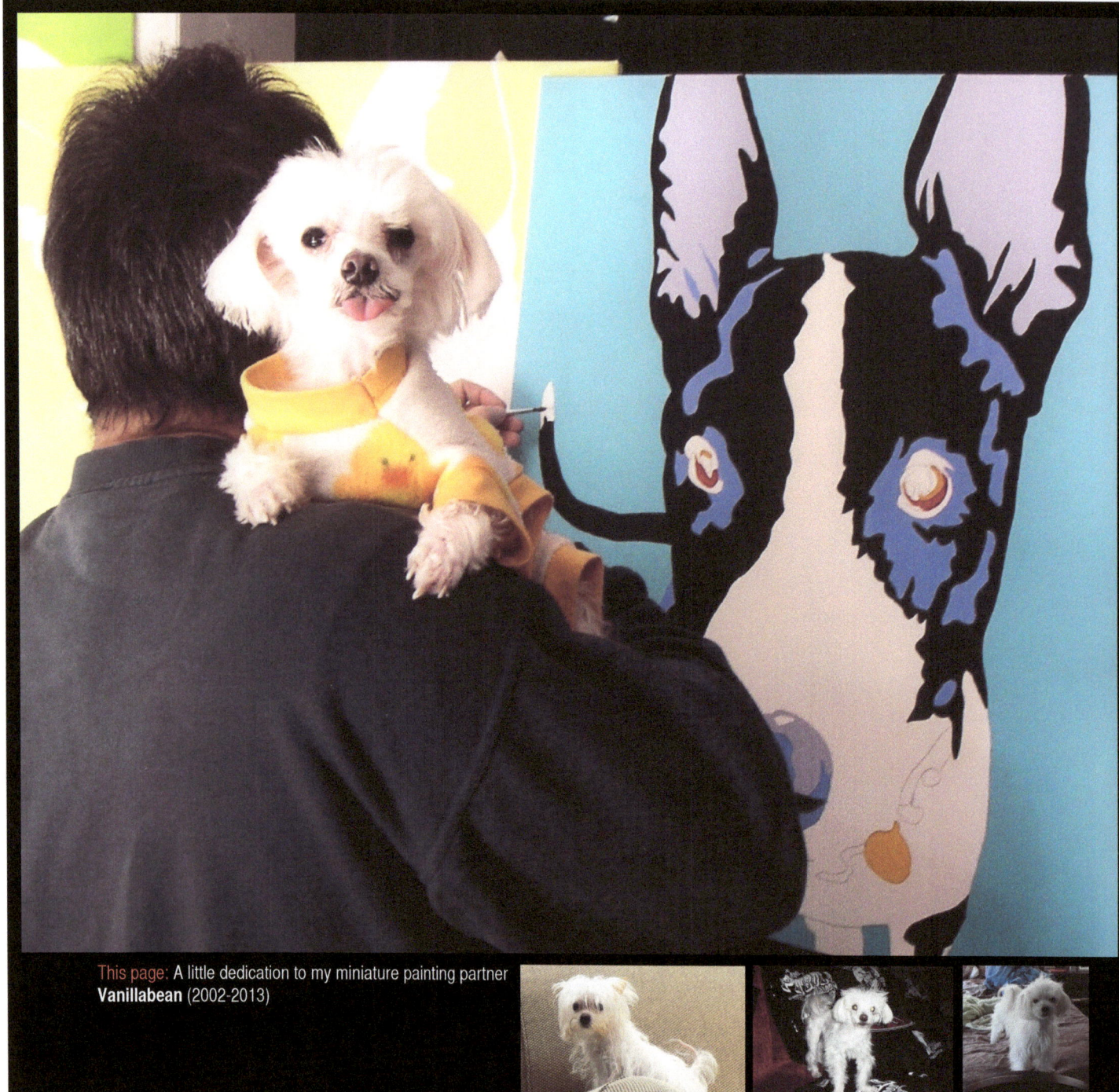

This page: A little dedication to my miniature painting partner **Vanillabean** (2002-2013)

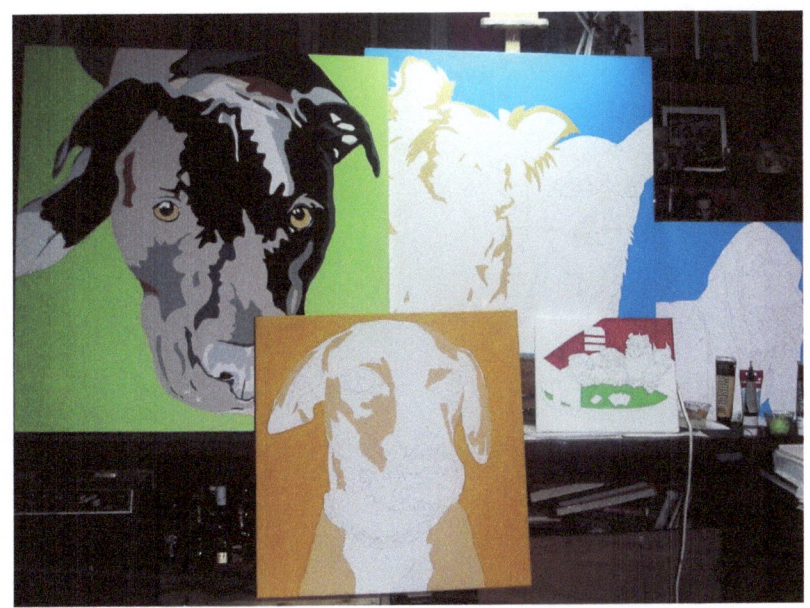

See all of Tommy's paintings, and have your own personal portrait commissioned, at

www.TommyPopArt.com

About the Artist

Tommy Athanasiou is a graduate of The Ducret School of Art, Plainfield, NJ and has been a creative art director and illustrator in NYC and South Florida for the past 28 years. He is an accomplished painter specializing in pop-art-style pet portraits (www.TommyPopArt.com), and is the creator of www.PitbullShirt.com, which features pitbull-positive clothing and accessories. 10% of all T-shirt proceeds are donated to non-profit pitbull rescues each month. He also is the author/illustrator of the *Peanut The Pitbull* children's book series.

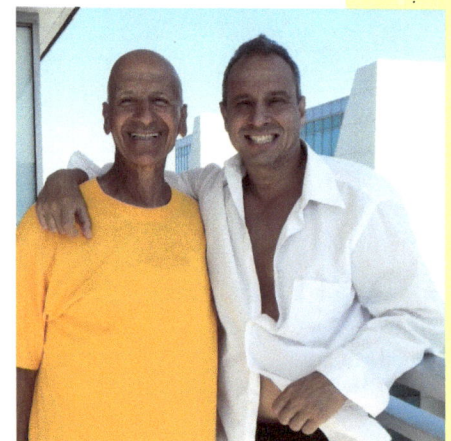

**Tommy and
his Dad**
August 2015

Tommy lives in South Florida with his wife Sharon, their adopted snuggly-goofy-lovebug pitbull girl named Peanut, a distinguished and sometimes too-smart-for-his-own-good toy poodle named Fluffernutter, and a recently adopted maltese named Melody Bean who loves to mimic a twirling ballerina when she's extra happy.

Photo Credits

Page 52
Tommy with Basil Gogos, Ricou Browning - **Jamil Malik**
Page 56
Carolie Manzo - **Becky Lyn Tegze**
Sally Kellerman
Shawn Marion - **Miguel Starcevich www.miguelphoto.com**
Tommy and *PIT BOSS* cast - **Frankie Rodriguez**
Page 57
Kristen Bauer - **Lionel Deluy www.LionelDeluy.com**
Danny Trejo
Tommy with William Shatner - **Wizard World**
Norman Reedus
Scott Wilson - **Matt Reyes**

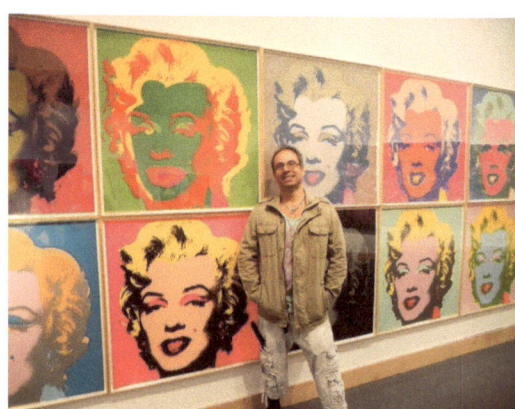

Boca Museum of Art
The complete Andy Warhol
Marilyn Monroe Screen Print Collection
February 2014

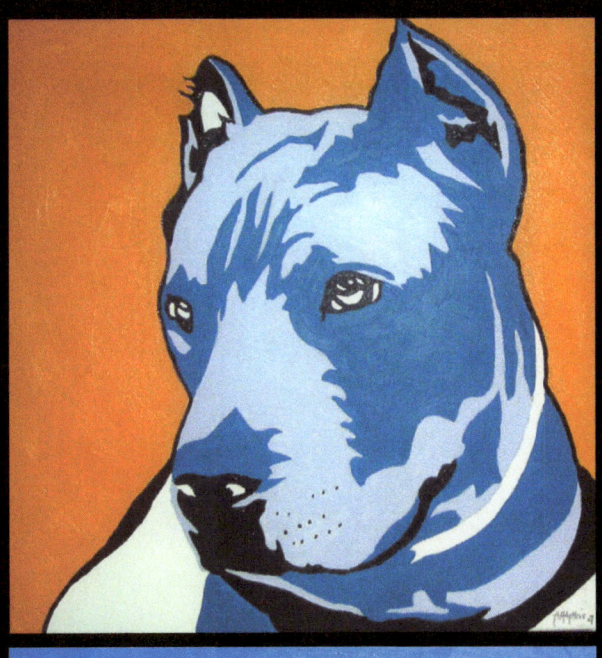
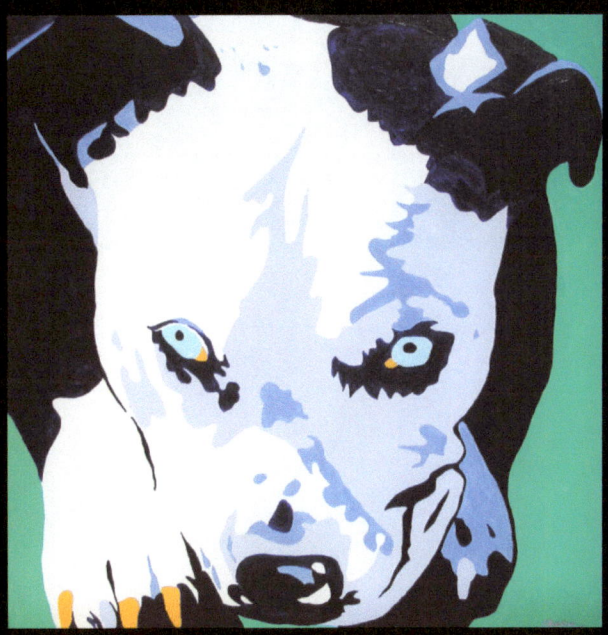
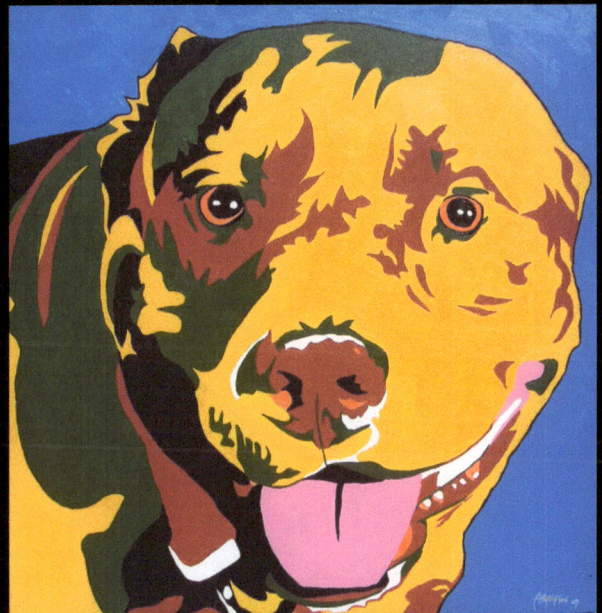
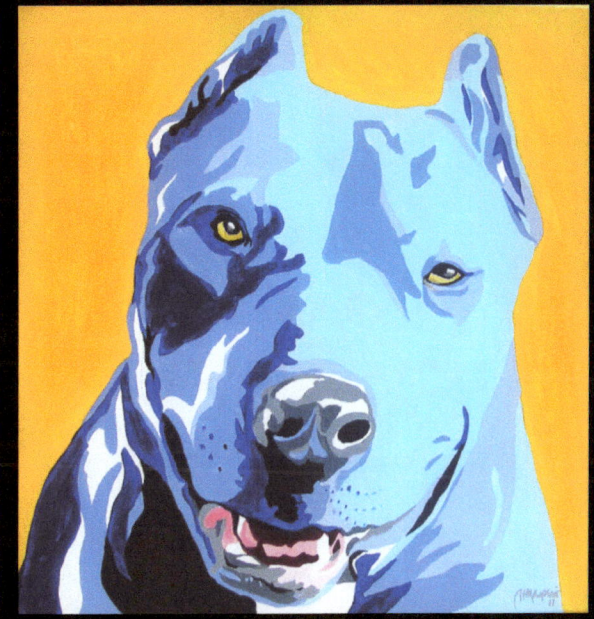

THE PITBULLS

TOMMY
POP
ART
.com

TOMMY**POP**ART.COM